© Copyright 1996 – European

THE FOUNDATION OF THE MODERN GREEK STATE
MAJOR TREATIES AND CONVENTIONS
(1830-1947)

MINISTRY OF FOREIGN AFFAIRS OF GREECE
SERVICE OF HISTORICAL ARCHIVES

THE FOUNDATION OF THE MODERN GREEK STATE

MAJOR TREATIES AND CONVENTIONS
(1830 - 1947)

RESEARCHED & EDITED BY
PHOTINI CONSTANTOPOULOU

KASTANIOTIS EDITIONS
ATHENS 1999

PROLOGUE: *George A. Papandreou.*

INTRODUCTION, INTRODUCTORY NOTES, TIME CHART, INDEX:
Photini Constantopoulou.

EDITING: *Photini Constantopoulou.*

EDITING ASSISTANTS: *Stella Kyriakou, Ioannis Begos & Stelios Zachariou.*

KASTANIOTIS EDITIONS S.A.
11, Zalongou St., GR-106 78 Athens
☎ 330.12.08 - 330.13.27 FAX: 384.24.31

ISBN 960-03-2506-5

CONTENTS

FOREWORD

———•⋯⋙◆◆◈⋘⋯•———

THE CONCLUSION of the Cold War has resulted in the creation of a new diplomatic environment. The lack of stability and political predictability have allowed history, perhaps more today than ever before, to claim unforeseen rights. Above all, the study of history as an imperative, with selected thematic targets, based on primary archival sources, remains a task of the highest priority for the Service of Historical Archives of the Hellenic Ministry of Foreign Affairs.

The present study is the outcome of intensive research into legal documents. It aims to inform citizens, diplomats, journalists and politicians of the historical developments which culminated in the formation of the modern Greek state. The goal of this publication is to present, for the first time in this context, the international treaties and protocols which determined the evolution of the frontiers of modern Greece. The long road towards the formation of the Greek nation-state within the framework of international politics forms the major theme of this study.

SERVICE OF HISTORICAL ARCHIVES

PROLOGUE

THE STUDY and publication of hitherto widely scattered documents relating to modern Greek diplomatic history initiated by the Service of Historical Archives of the Hellenic Ministry of Foreign Affairs, fulfils a goal of great historical importance. It is also, however, of particular relevance to present circumstances. The international treaties and conventions of which this volume is comprised document the 'tortured' history of the Modern Greek State, from its foundation to the final establishment of its present borders. At the same time, they constitute an effective tool for the exercise of Greek foreign policy.

The texts of international conventions are far more an expression of the balance of power on the morrow of major historical events: they embody the fundamental principles governing the international behaviour of states, and sustain a solid achievement in the context of the implementation of International Law. The territorial integrity and the inviolability of national borders represent the kind of principles on which relations of peaceful co-existence and co-operation between states and peoples can be erected.

Many will dispute and call into question the validity of International Law and the credibility of international organisations in the present transitional phase of international politics. What should be stressed is that in the 21st century, international relations will have to be conducted on the basis of the overriding force of International Law: otherwise we run the risk of entering upon an extended period of barbarism and anarchy throughout the world. History has taught us that war breaks out every time revisionary forces attempt to overturn the international status quo.

Greek foreign policy is formulated on the basis of respect for the principles of International Law and international treaties. It is a policy of peaceful co-existence and co-operation. A policy of strength, not weakness.

Athens, 22 July 1999
GEORGE A. PAPANDREOU
Minister of Foreign Affairs

INTRODUCTION

THE UNIFICATION of Greece within the frontiers of the modern Greek state was an undertaking which lasted for more than a century. The fact that Greek populations dwelt outside the borders[1] of what is now Greece and the natural fragmentation of the country with its numerous islands were factors which impeded the process of unification. On the other hand, the language, religion and awareness of a common cultural heritage[2] which the Greeks cultivated in their schools,[3] proved to be powerful factors in post-revolutionary state-building.

The struggle for Independence was heralded by the work of Rhigas Velestinlis and the *Philike Etaireia* in the Danubian principalities. The undertaking was encouraged by Russia's influence in the Balkan Peninsula and its protection of the Christian popula-

---

1. According to Dakin, many Greeks lived in the regions around the Black Sea and in the Danubian principalities, in Constantinople, where they accounted for 300,000 inhabitants out of a total population of 880,000, and Asia Minor, where the Greek population numbered approximately 1,800,000 (D. Dakin, *The Unification of Greece, 1770-1923*, London: Ernest Benn, 1972). There were also Greek communities in Egypt, Palestine and North Africa.

2. Throughout the Byzantine period, and during the dynasties of the Comneni and Palaiologi emperors in particular, devotion to the spirit of the Classical era continued with only brief interruptions. The Greek scholars who took refuge in the West after the fall of Constantinople introduced classical ideas into the European Enlightenment, which in turn had an impact on the Greeks as they fought for their freedom in 1821.

3. During the period of Ottoman rule, secret schools in which young Greeks were taught by the clergy functioned at night in churches.

tions under the Ottoman yoke. Yet, the idea of a pan-Balkan rising failed, and the struggle soon passed into the hands of the armed captains of central and southern Greece. Metropolitan Bishop Germanos of Patras raised the standard of struggle against the Ottomans and proclaimed the outbreak of the Greek War of Independence on 25 March 1821.[4]

After numerous land and sea battles, the War of Independence became consolidated. The cause won the support of many European liberals and intellectuals,[5] at a particularly difficult time for revolutionary movements, when the prevailing spirit was that of the Holy Alliance and Austrian Foreign Minister Kl. Metternich.

On 1 January 1822, the First National Assembly, meeting at Epidaurus, proclaimed 'before God and man' the political existence and Independence of the Greek nation. By 1823, the Revolution had gathered momentum, reinforced by victories on land[6] and at sea.[7] In 1825 Ibrahim Pasha, the son of Mehmet Ali of Egypt, authorised by the Ottoman Sultan to put down the Greek revolution, landed in the Peloponnese with a powerful army.[8] The legendary

---

4. 25 March is the Greek national holiday.

5. Among the most eminent Philhellenes, who contributed actively to the struggle for freedom, were Lord Byron, Leicester Stanhope, George Finlay, Jean G. Eynard, Santore Santarosa and Charles Fabvier. The British were the first to develop philhellenic activities (representatives of the London Greek Committee), followed by the French in Paris (Société philanthropique en faveur des Grecs, Société de la morale chrétienne) and Marseille. Philhellenic committees were also set up in Geneva, the Netherlands, Sweden and the United States (Philadelphia, New York, Boston), where President James Monroe declared himself in favour of the Greek War of Independence, a stance which was in harmony with his doctrine of supporting free and independent nation-states.

6. Such as the destruction of the army under Dramali Pasha by the Greek captain, Theodoros Kolokotronis.

7. Including the burning of the Turkish flagship by Admiral Constantinos Kanaris, another hero of the War of Independence.

8. On 12 February 1825, Ibrahim landed 4,000 troops and 500 cavalry. C. Paparrigopoulos, *History of the Greek Nation*, Vol. 6, p. 125, 1872, (in Greek).

commander of the Greek forces, Theodoros Kolokotronis, responded with guerrilla warfare. In the same year, the blockade and siege of Mesolonghi began. The fall of the town, and the heroic exodus of its defenders, awakened the conscience of Europe. The philhellenic current grew in strength influencing the governments of the European Powers which gradually showed interest in the Greek question. In 1826 Great Britain, under the premiership of George Canning, and Russia, under Tsar Nicholas, signed the St. Petersburg Protocol, to which France acceded later. France's accession led to the signature of the London Treaty (July 1827). Both agreements were directly associated with the naval battle of Navarino (1827), which resulted in the destruction of the Egyptian and Turkish fleets.

When Count Ioannis Capodistrias, the first President of Greece,[9] arrived and formed a government (1828), the people were starving and exhausted, and Greece lacked any form of organisation and administration. The Ottomans, moreover, still held certain key positions in southern and central Greece. The arrival of Capodistrias restored the rule of law and public order, and the first steps were taken towards organising the administration, education and economy of the country. During this period, the European Powers were deeply involved in the domestic affairs of Greece. Capodistrias knew well that the obstacles to the creation of an independent state –the state which the Greeks so fervently desired– would be formidable. It was for this reason that the President placed great emphasis from the outset on the diplomatic readiness of Greece. Circumventing conflicts of interest and political influence, he applied a policy of equal friendship with all three Powers and prepared the first Greek notes of protest to the Royal Councils of Europe. The Russo-Turkish War (1828-1829) which broke out at this time had a decisive impact on the Greek cause, because it enabled the Greek army and fleet to redouble

---

9. He was elected to the post for a seven-year term by the National Assembly of Troezene in April 1827.

their efforts to drive the Ottoman forces out of Greece. After rounds of negotiations with the ambassadors of the Great Powers, the London Protocols of 16 November 1828 and 22 March 1829 were signed, leading ultimately to the protocol of 3 February 1830 by which the political Independence of Greece was triumphantly proclaimed and the borders were fixed at the Aspropotamos-Sperchios line.[10] The protocol of 1830 also declared that Leopold of Saxe-Coburg would become Prince-Sovereign of Greece.

Capodistrias was supported in his efforts by Leopold - who, however, in disagreement with the European Powers and for personal reasons, refused the Greek crown. His refusal and a change of government in London[11] caused a shift in British policy regarding the northern frontiers of Greece. In the meantime, the continued endeavours of Capodistrias to set the Greek state on its feet and his fruitless efforts to bring about a rapprochement with his political opponents[12] led to his assassination on 9 October 1831. Yet, he was vindicated in the finalisation of the borders and his policy of delaying the evacuation of Acarnania and Aetolia. The London Conference of July 1831 acknowledged the serious defects of the protocol of 3 February 1830 and its failure to provide means of establishing mutual security between the Ottoman Empire and the new Greek state. For that reason, British diplomacy (Stratford Canning) sought an improvement in the Greek frontiers and suggested the adoption of the previously consented Arta-Volos line.

---

10. This new dividing line was far less favourable to Greece than that granted by the March 1829 protocol, because it left the greater part of western central Greece outside the frontiers of the country. On this point, the Great Powers gave way to the Ottoman Empire in exchange for an understanding that the latter would accept the political Independence of Greece.

11. The new administration was headed by Charles Grey as Prime Minister with Lord Palmerston as Foreign Secretary.

12. The opposition accused Capodistrias of having caused the withdrawal of Leopold, claiming that the Greek President was not only devoted to, but also completely dependent upon Russia.

The London Protocol of 13 February 1832, which contributed a comprehensive solution of the Greek question, included the decision of the Great Powers that Otto (in Greek, Othon), Prince of Bavaria, would become King of Greece. On 26 April 1832, De Cetto, the Bavarian plenipotentiary in London, submitted a memorandum to the London Conference calling for the Greek frontier to be moved further north, running from the Ambracian Gulf to the Aegean. Finally, the London Protocol of 30 August 1832 awarded Greece the area around Lamia,[13] but the Cretan request for union with Greece was dismissed while the island of Samos was granted autonomy.[14]

The hopes generated by the arrival of Othon in Greece in 1833 were undermined during the Bavarian Regency by political squabbling, conflicts among family-based factions, and the open intervention of the Great Powers in domestic affairs. Such interventionism continued even after Othon attained his majority on 1 June 1835. Throughout Othon's reign, Greece remained within the borders secured by the War of Independence. The refusal of the Greek monarch to grant the country a constitution, in conjunction with the fact that he had produced no heir, resulted in civil unrest and even open rebellion. The chain reaction of civilian upheaval focused on the demand for a constitution.

The improvement in the system of governance established by the adoption of a constitution in 1844 generated the alternation of the pro-Russian, pro-British and pro-French parties in power until Othon was forced to abdicate in 1862.

In the meantime, the Eastern Question had entered a new phase of crisis and its impact was felt in Greece. Hopes that the

---

13. The report of the border commission, which completed the delineation of the Greek-Turkish border from the Ambracian Gulf to the Pagasitic Gulf, was submitted on 25 November 1832.

14. Samos was declared a self-governing principality under a Christian Prince, who would be a tributary of the Sultan.

unredeemed Greeks would attain liberation led to small-scale risings in Thessaly, Macedonia and Epirus. This sequence of uprisings ended with the suppression of a revolution in Crete (1841). This period further defined the rise of the 'Great Idea', an ideology which dominated the country's foreign policy for decades and had both positive and negative effects on Greece's future. The outbreak of the Crimean War (1854) triggered a fresh wave of enthusiasm and generated new hopes for the Greeks. It was widely believed that Othon planned to cross the Greek-Turkish borders, and assume the leadership of the revolutionaries in Thessaly. Under pressure from Britain and France, the monarch was compelled to make a statement of neutrality before the Senate on 26 May 1854. However, this did not prevent the outbreak of risings in Epirus, Thessaly and Macedonia.

A sequence of domestic crises soon broke out. In 1857, an international commission was installed to control the country's public finances and remained in place until the London Protocol of 6 June 1863, which placed Prince William of Denmark on the throne as George I. One month later (13 July 1863), Britain, France and Russia confirmed the King's coming of age and undertook to settle the obligations which they had assumed as early as 1830. The fifteen articles of the treaty also dealt with the enlargement of the state borders through the cession of the Ionian Islands to Greece.[15]

During the first eighteen years of the reign of George I, the union of the Ionian Islands to Greece, and the annexation[16] of Thessaly and the Arta area increased the size of Greece from 47,516 square kilometres in 1832 to 63,606 square kilometres in 1881. The

---

15. By the London Treaty of 14 November 1863 the five Great Powers (Austria, Prussia, Russia, Britain, France) officialy declared Britain's withdrawal from the protection of the Ionian Islands. Finally, by the treaty of 29 March 1864 the details of unification were settled and the Greek flag was raised over the castles of the Ionian Islands on 2 June 1864.

16. By the Convention of Constantinople of 2 July 1881.

country acquired a new constitution in 1864 and considerable progress was made in the economic and social sectors. There were, however, still difficulties, and party political expediencies were ever-present. Between 1866 and 1869, a rebellion occurred in Crete; Greece and the Ottoman Empire broke off diplomatic relations, and another war between the two countries seemed almost inevitable. During the 1860s' Greece found itself involved for the first time in a confrontation with another Christian-Orthodox Balkan nation, the Bulgarians. Superficially, the dispute between the two countries was over ecclesiastical matters, concerning the establishment of an autocephalous Bulgarian Church which was not dependent on the Oecumenical Patriarchate. In reality, however, this was an international dispute, which centered on the question of future control over the Ottoman lands in Macedonia and Thrace. Behind the aspirations of the Bulgarian nationalists –lay and clerical– were the expansionist ambitions of Russia: pan-Slavism, encouraged by Russian policy, posed a grave challenge to the Greek state.

The revolts in Bosnia-Hercegovina (1875) marked the beginning of a new phase in the Eastern Question, and the adverse climate for the Ottoman Empire was further exacerbated by a rebellion in Bulgaria (1876) and by a war with Serbia (1876). However, the Constantinople Conference of 1876 was a dual disappointment for the Greeks, since it was clear that Russia favoured the formation of a Greater Bulgaria, while Britain and the other European Powers displayed general indifference towards the fate of those Greek inhabited regions which were still under Ottoman rule.

War between Russia and the Ottoman Empire broke out in 1877-1878, and the Greek army entered Thessaly, though without a formal declaration of war. Crete, too, rose in revolt. Internal weakness and indecisiveness prevented Greece from gaining territorial benefits. However, the European Powers were strengthened in their resolve to move the Greek frontier further north, in order to prevent the annexation of Macedonian territory by Bulgaria. The Ottoman Empire, now weakened, was led from San Stefano[17] to the European Congress of Berlin (13 July 1878).[18]

The Congress of Berlin established the autonomous province of Eastern Rumelia. Now negotiations focused on Macedonia - which was still under Ottoman rule and for which the International Commission proposed a draft administrative reform plan in late 1880 - and Crete. In the case of the latter, the Halepa Pact concerning the islands' administration was signed in 1878. A conference –held in Constantinople after a series of incidents which almost led to renewed war between Greece and the Ottoman Empire– resulted in the decision that Thessaly and the Arta area would be annexed to the Kingdom of Greece (Treaty of Constantinople, 24 May 1881). For the first time since Independence, Greece had succeeded in redeeming from the Ottoman Empire territories inhabited by Greeks and incorporating them into the Hellenic Kingdom.

In 1896, Crete rose in revolt once again, over the failure of the Ottomans to comply with the terms of the Halepa Pact. Although attempts were made to find a solution, and despite the intervention of the European Powers, this time a Greek-Turkish war was not avoided. It ended in serious defeat for Greece, which by the armistice agreement of 20 May 1897 was compelled to pay compensation of four million Turkish pounds to the Ottomans. Furthermore, under the interim peace agreement of 18 September 1897, Greece submitted its finances to the scrutiny of an inter-

---

17. The Treaty of San Stefano, 3 March 1878, calling for the creation of a large Bulgarian State.

18. Greek involvement in the Congress was the wish of Britain, which hoped to use the Greek demands to restrict the influence of Russian policy in the Balkans. However, Greece played no part in the settlement of its territorial question, since its delegation was excluded from the crucial decision-making process of the Congress. The Greek delegation was told it would be allowed to present its views only at the discussions on the fate of Epirus, Thessaly and Crete.

national commission, in order to receive a foreign loan out of which the reparations would be paid. Thanks mainly to the insistence of Queen Victoria, Greece was able to avoid a frontier change which would have reduced its territory. A major matter still outstanding between Greece and the Ottoman Empire, after the signature of the Peace Treaty in Constantinople (December 1897) which finalised the provisions of the interim aggreement of September, was Crete and the question of its status. The Powers decided (1898) that the supreme authority should be vested in a High Commissioner of their choice, who proved to be Prince George, second son of the Greek King.

The Eastern Question had by now entered a new phase, with Bulgaria casting covetous eyes on Macedonia. The region, located at the centre of the European part of the Ottoman Empire, was inhabited mainly by Christians of ethnicities akin to all the states of the Balkan peninsula. The ambitious plans of Ferdinand of Bulgaria, who sought to play a central role in the Balkans similar to that of the Prussian Emperor, were assisted by the 'Internal Macedonian Revolutionary Organisation' (IMRO), founded in Sofia, calling for Macedonian autonomy. Indeed, in 1899 Bulgaria appealed to the Sultan, requesting the formal autonomy of Macedonia, with Thessaloniki as its capital and a Christian governor. The activities of the Bulgarian-backed *comitadji* guerrillas in the area caused a deterioration in relations among all the Christian populations of the Balkans.

The recognition of Bulgarian independence and the nationalist Young Turk coup d' état of 1908 were sources of great concern for Greece. In October 1908, the decision of the Assembly of Crete to declare union with Greece almost triggered a new Greek-Turkish war. In September 1911, however, the ambitions of Rome in North Africa caused a war between Italy and the Ottomans, and the former, not content with the conquest and annexation of Tripolitania and Cyrenaica in North Africa, landed troops in the Dodecanese. By the peace treaty of 15 October 1912 (signed at Ouchy, Lausanne), the Ottoman Empire succumbed to the Italian demand that it evacuate these North African territories, but refused to relinquish the Dodecanese.

The concern and fear caused by the Young Turk nationalist movement brought about a rapprochement among the Balkan states. After concluding various treaties of alliance and defensive pacts, the four Balkan states –Greece, Serbia, Bulgaria and Montenegro– launched an offensive against the Ottomans in the Balkans. The First Balkan War ended with the London Peace Treaty of 30 May 1913, according to which the Balkan allies gained all the territory to the west of the Enos-Midia line. The Great Powers undertook to decide the fate of the Aegean islands[19] and Crete.

Bulgaria's reluctance to co-operate with Greece, Serbia and Roumania over the division of Macedonia was the cause of the Second Balkan War. Bulgaria was defeated by the combined forces of the other Balkan states and was compelled to sign the Peace Treaty of Bucharest (10 August 1913) as a result of which Greece doubled its territory and increased its population by two million people. Now Greece occupied a central position, both in the network of relations in the Balkans and in the European balance of political and military power.

Despite initial enthusiasm, Greek victories in the Balkan Wars and the country's unprecedented expansion soon gave rise to fears of future conflict with Bulgaria and the Ottoman Empire. Prime Minister Eleftherios Venizelos, therefore, adopted a moderate attitude towards Greece's differences with its neighbours, and accepted the proposal of the Great Powers (13 February 1914) that the islands of the Aegean –with the exception of Imbros, Tenedos

---

19. Italy refused to cede the Dodecanese to Greece on the pretext that it was obliged to hand the islands back to the Sultan. In fact, however, it wished to use them as a bargaining counter to extend the borders of Albania as far as Ioannina.

and Castellorizo– would be ceded to Greece on the condition that the Greek Army withdrew from Albania. Although 'Northern Epirus' (Southern Albania) was declared autonomous, the Greek army withdrew from the above area by mid-April 1914.

Eleftherios Venizelos dominated Greek politics from 1910 to the inter-War period. He has been credited for the expansion of Greece's territory and for bringing the country into World War I on to the side of the victors, although at the expense of clashing with King Constantine. The disastrous campaign in Asia Minor culminated in the expulsion of 1.5 million Greeks from Turkey in 1922-23. The period from 1923 to 1933 was a time of deténte in the Balkans, when attempts were made to improve relations and eliminate hostility.[20]

In 1933, the rise to power of the Nazis in Germany altered the situation in Europe and pushed the Balkan states into pacts of co-operation. The political crisis in Greece which, on 4 August 1936, led to the establishment of a dictatorship under Ioannis Metaxas, coincided with a series of international crises throughout the continent. The 'August Fourth' regime (1936-1941) based its foreign policy on strengthening the bonds between Greece and Britain, but Metaxas also took care to maintain good relations with the other Balkan countries in order to counter Italian expansionism. The torpedoing by an Italian submarine of the Greek cruiser *Elli* on 15 August 1940 brought to a head the Italian campaign of provocation against Greece. A few months later, Metaxas dismissed an Italian ultimatum with a terse 'No' ('Ochi') and Italy declared war on Greece. The Greek Army's victories on the Albanian front and its advance to Argyrokastro and Korytsa were a serious embarrassment to Mussolini, as it provided the first victories against the Axis Powers. By early 1941, however, Hitler

---

20. Bulgaria, following a revisionist policy at the time, did not participate in these efforts of Balkan co-operation. Despite this antithesis, a kind of tacit truce had come about between the European Powers involved in the Balkans.

would come to the rescue of his ally and through 'Operation Marita' quickly overtake Greece. The heroic resistance of the Greek people contributed decisively to the outcome of the War and the defeat of the Axis Powers.[21] Greece suffered losses proportionately greater than any of the belligerent states[22] and the treaty signed in Paris (1947) resulted in the Italian-held, but Greek-populated, Dodecanese islands becoming part of Greece.

After the War, the economic reconstruction of Greece was achieved by the Greek people with the support and assistance provided by the Marshall Plan. During the decades which followed, Greece joined the North Atlantic Treaty Organisation (1952), and subsequently, the European Community, becoming an associate member in 1962, and a full member in 1981. Thus, the borders of Greece also became the borders of Europe.

PHOTINI CONSTANTOPOULOU
Director,
Service of Historical Archives

---

21. See *Greece's involvement in the Second World War*, Vols. A-B-C, Academy of Athens, 1998, (in Greek).

22. An analysis of the war damages suffered by Greece can be found in the report presented by the Greek delegation at the '*London Conference on Nazi Gold*', Lancaster House, 2-4 December 1997.

19TH CENTURY:

From the War of Independence
to the Annexation of Thessaly and the Arta Area

LONDON PROTOCOL

(3 February 1830)

ALTHOUGH IT *has come to be known as 'the London Protocol', the text actually consists of three protocols, signed in London by the pleni-potentiaries of Great Britain, France and Russia. The first declared the Independence of Greece, under a monarchy, and determined the borders of the country; the second concerned the choice of Prince Leopold of Saxe-Coburg as Prince-Sovereign of Greece and the third, drawn up at the request of France, established religious toleration and retained in force all the privileges which the Latin Church had hitherto enjoyed in the former Ottoman provinces from which the independent Greek state was created. The signature of these protocols, and, indeed, Greek Indepen-dence itself, were the outcome of the destruction of the Ottoman and Egyptian fleets in Navarino harbour on 20 October 1827, an event which led to negotiations in Constantinople among the ambassadors of Britain, France and Russia on the one hand and the Sultan on the other. The refusal of the Sultan to accept the terms of the London Treaty of 6 July 1827, which inter alia was the corner-stone of Greek Independence, resulted in the withdrawal of the three ambassadors from Constantinople in late 1827. Without making any mention of borders, the treaty provided for the establishment of economic relations with Greece and the appointment of consuls. Ultimately, the consequences of the Russo-Turkish war which followed, the decisions reached at the conferences of Poros (autumn-December 1828) and London, leading to the signature of a protocol on 22 March 1829, and the provisions of the Treaty of Adria-nople (14 September 1829),[1] all paved the way for renewed negotiations*

---

1. With the Adrianople (Edirne) Peace Treaty between Russia and the Ottoman Empire, which brought to an end the war between the two countries, the Porte

between the Porte and the three Great Powers (Britain, France and Russia). These talks finally resulted in the signature of the three texts collectively known as the London Protocol of 1830.

---

proclaimed its full consent to the Treaty of London (July 1827). That treaty had recognised Greece as a tributary state to the Sultan, with complete freedom of internal administration, trade and religion and with a government elected –under certain conditions– by the Greeks. By the Treaty of Adrianople, the Ottoman Empire also recognised the London Protocol of 22 March 1829, which addressed the delineation of the frontiers of the new state and the amount of tribute to be paid to the Sultan. Britain did not accept the solution to the Greek question which was being promoted, in the belief that recognition of an entirely independent new state in the East would create problems. This recognition was not achieved until the London Protocol of 3 February 1830.

Protocole* (No 1) tenu à Londres le 3 Février 1830, relatif à l'indépendance de la Grèce.

—◦◦◦—

Présents: les Plénipotentiaires de Russie, de France et de la Grande-Bretagne.

Les Plénipotentiaires des trois Cours s'étant réunis au Département des affaires étrangères,

A l'ouverture de la conférence, le Plénipotentiaire de Sa Majesté Britannique et celui de Sa Majesté très chrétienne témoignent au Plénipotentiaire de Sa Majesté Impériale le désir de savoir sous quel point de vue il envisage l'art. 10 du traité signé récemment à Adrinople entre la Russie et l'Empire Ottoman, article qui a rapport aux affaires de la Grèce.

Les Plénipotentiaires de Sa Majesté Impériale déclarent que l'art.10 du traité en question n'invalide pas les droits des alliés de l'Empereur, n'entrave pas les délibérations des Ministres réunis en conférence à Londres, et ne met aucun obstacle aux arrangements que les trois Cours jugeraient d'un commun accord être les plus utiles et les mieux adaptés aux circonstances.

A la suite de cette déclaration, le Plénipotentiaire de Sa Majesté Britannique fait part à la Conférence d'une dépêche collective, ci-jointe sub.Lit.A., par laquelle les Ambassadeurs de la France et de la Grande-Bretagne à Constantinople transmettent une déclaration de la Porte Ottomane, en date du 9 septembre, également ci-jointe sub.Lit.B., et qui annonce que la Porte, ayant

---

* G. Noradoungian, *Recueil d'Actes Internationaux de l' Empire Ottoman: 1789-1856*, 2ème tome, Paris: Cottilon, 1900, pp. 177-181.

déjà adhéré au traité de Londres, promet et s'engage de plus aujourd'hui, vis-à-vis des Représentants des Puissances signataires dudit traité, à souscrire entièrement à toutes les déterminations que prendra la Conférence de Londres relativement à son exécution. La lecture de ce document fait unanimement reconnaître l'obligation où se trouve l'Alliance de procéder, avant tout, à l'établissement immédiat de l'armistice sur terre et sur mer, entre les Turcs et les Grecs.

Il est résolu, en conséquence, que les Plénipotentiaires des trois Cours à Constantinople, leurs Résidents en Grèce et leurs Amiraux dans l'Archipel recevront sans délai l'ordre de réclamer et d'obtenir des parties contendantes une prompte et entière cessation d'hostilités.

A cet effet, des instructions ci-annexées sub.Lit.C.D.E. ont été concertées et arrêtées pour les dits Plénipotentiaires et Résidents, ainsi que pour les trois Amiraux, le rétablissement de la paix entre la Russie et la Porte permettant à l'Amiral russe de reprendre part aux opérations de ses collègues d'Angleterre et de France.

Ces premières déterminations convenues, les membres de la Conférence trouvant que les déclarations Ottomanes les mettent dans le cas de concerter les mesures qui leur paraissent préférables d'adopter dans l'état actuel des choses, et désirant apporter aux dispositions antérieures de l'Alliance les améliorations les plus propres à assurer de nouveaux gages de stabilité à l'œuvre de paix dont Elle s'occupe, ont, d'un commun accord, arrêté les clauses suivantes:

1. La Grèce formera un Etat indépendant, et jouira de tous les droits politiques, administratifs, et commerciaux, attachés à une indépendance complète.

2. En considération de ces avantages accordés au nouvel Etat, et pour déférer au désir qu'a exprimé la Porte d'obtenir la réduction des frontières fixées par le protocole du 22 mars, la ligne de démarcation des limites de la Grèce partira de l'embouchure du fleuve de l'Aspropotamos, remontera ce fleuve jusqu'à la

hauteur du lac d'Anghelocastro, et, traversant ce lac, ainsi que ceux de Vrachori et de Saurovitza, elle aboutira au mont Artotina, d'où elle suivra la crête du mont Oxas, la vallée de Calouri et la crête du mont Œta, jusqu'au golfe de Zeitoun, qu'elle atteindra à l'embouchure du Sperchius.

Tous les territoires et pays situés au sud de cette ligne, que la Conférence a indiqués sur la carte ci-jointe, appartiendront à la Grèce, et tous les pays et territoires situés au Nord de cette même ligne continueront à faire partie de l'Empire Ottoman.

Appartiendront également à la Grèce, l'île de Négrepont tout entière avec les îles du Diable et l'île Skyro, et les îles connues anciennement sous le nom de Cyclades, y compris l'île d'Amorgo, situées entre le 38me et 39me degré de latitude Nord, et le 26me de longitude Est, du méridien de Greenwich.

3. Le Gouvernement de la Grèce sera monarchique et héréditaire, par ordre de primogéniture. Il sera confié à un Prince qui ne pourra pas être choisi parmi ceux des familles régnantes dans les Etats signataires du traité du 6 juillet 1827, et portera le titre de Prince Souverain de la Grèce. Le choix de ce Prince fera l'objet de communications et de stipulations ultérieures.

4. Aussitôt que les clauses du présent protocole auront été portées à la connaissance des parties intéressées, la paix entre l'Empire Ottoman et la Grèce sera sensée rétablie *ipso facto,* et les sujets des deux Etats seront traités réciproquement, sous le rapport des droits de commerce et de navigation, comme ceux des autres Etats en paix avec l'Empire Ottoman et la Grèce.

5. Des actes d'amnistie pleine et entière seront immédia-tement publiés par la Porte Ottomane et par le Gouvernement grec.

L'acte d'amnistie de la Porte proclamera qu'aucun Grec, dans toute l'étendue de ses domaines, ne pourra être privé de ses propriétés, ni inquiété aucunement, à raison de la part qu'il aura prise à l'insurrection de la Grèce. L'acte d'amnistie du gouver-nement grec proclamera le même principe en faveur de tous les Musulmans ou Chrétiens qui auraient pris parti contre sa cause; et il sera de plus entendu et publié que les Musulmans qui voudraient continuer à habiter les territoires et îles assignés à la Grèce, y conserveront leurs propriétés, et y jouiront invariablement, avec leurs familles, d'une sécurité parfaite.

6. La Porte Ottomane accordera à ceux de ses sujets Grecs qui désireraient quitter le territoire turc, un délai d'un an pour vendre leurs propriétés et sortir librement du pays.

Le Gouvernement grec laissera la même faculté aux habitants de la Grèce qui voudraient se transporter sur le territoire turc.

7.Toutes les forces grecques de terre et de mer évacueront les territoires, places et îles qu'elles occupent au delà de la ligne assignée aux limites de la Grèce dans le para. 2, et se retireront derrière cette ligne dans le plus bref délai. Toutes les forces turques de terre et de mer qui occupent des territoires, places ou îles, compris dans les limites mentionnées ci-dessus, évacueront ces îles, places et territoires, et se retireront derrière les dites limites, et pareillement dans le plus bref délai.

8. Chacune des trois Cours conservera la faculté que lui assure l'art. 4 du traité du 6 juillet 1827, de garantir l'ensemble des arrangements et clauses qui précèdent. Les actes de garantie, s'il y en a, seront dressés séparément. L'action et les effets de ces divers actes deviendront, conséquemment à l'article susdit, l'objet de stipulations ultérieures des Hautes Puissances.

Aucune troupe appartenant à l'une des trois Puissances contractantes ne pourra entrer sur le territoire du nouvel Etat grec, sans l'assentiment des deux autres Cours signataires du traité.

9. Afin d'éviter les collisions qui ne manqueraient pas de résulter, dans les circonstances actuelles, d'un contrat entre les commissaires démarcateurs Ottomans, et les commissaires démarcateurs Grecs, quand il s'agira d'arrêter sur les lieux le tracé des frontières de la Grèce, il est convenu que ce travail sera confié à des Commissaires britanniques, français et russes, et que chacune des trois Cours en nommera un. Ces Commissaires, munis d'une

instruction, qui se trouve ci-jointe sub. Lit. G., arrêteront le tracé des dites frontières, en suivant, avec toute l' exactitude possible la ligne indiquée dans le para. 2, marqueront cette ligne par des poteaux, et en dresseront deux cartes, signées par eux, dont l'une sera remise au Gouvernement Ottoman, et l'autre au Gouvernement Grec.

Ils seront tenus d'achever leurs travaux dans l'espace de six mois. En cas de différence d'opinion entre les trois commissaires, la majorité des voix décidera.

10. Les dispositions du présent protocole seront immédiatement portées à la connaissance du Gouvernement Ottoman par les Plénipotentiaires des trois Cours, qui seront munis à cet effet d'une instruction commune ci-jointe sub.Lit.H. Les résidents des trois Cours en Grèce recevront aussi, sur le même sujet, l'instruction ci-jointe sub.Lit.I.

11. Les trois Cours se réservent de faire entrer les présentes stipulations dans un traité formel, qui sera signé à Londres, considéré comme exécutif de celui du 6 juillet 1827, et communiqué aux autres Cours de l'Europe, avec invitation d'y accéder, si elles le jugent convenable.

Conclusion. - Arrivés ainsi au terme d'une longue et difficile négociation, les trois Cours se félicitent sincèrement d'être parvenues à un parfait accord, au milieu des circonstances les plus graves et les plus délicates.

Le maintien de leur union dans de tels moments offre le meilleur gage de sa durée, et les trois Cours se flattent que cette union, stable autant que bienfaisante, ne cessera de contribuer à l'affermissement de la paix du monde.

(signé)
LIEVEN. MONTMORENCY-LAVAL. ABERDEEN.

TREATY (ARRANGEMENT) OF CONSTANTINOPLE

(21 July 1832)

This treaty was the product of the Constantinople Conference which opened in February 1832 with the participation of Great Britain, France and Russia on the one hand and the Ottoman Empire on the other. The factors which shaped the treaty included the refusal of Leopold to assume the Greek throne. He inter alia was not at all satisfied with the Aspropotamos-Zitouni borderline, which replaced the more favourable Arta-Volos line considered by the Great Powers earlier. The withdrawal of Leopold as a candidate for the throne of Greece, and the July revolution in France, delayed the final settlement of the frontiers of the new kingdom until a new government was formed in Britain. Lord Palmerston, who took over as British Foreign Secretary, agreed to the Arta-Volos borderline. However, the secret note[1] on Crete, which the Bavarian plenipotentiary communicated to the Courts of Britain, France and Russia, bore no fruit. Under the protocol signed on 7 May 1832 between Bavaria and the protecting Powers, and basically dealing with the way in which the Regency was to be managed until Othon reached his majority (while also concluding the second Greek loan, for a sum of £2,400,000 sterling), Greece was defined as an independent kingdom, with the Arta-Volos line as its northern frontier. This definition was reiterated in the London Protocol of 30 August 1832 signed

---

1. The secret note presented by the Bavarian Plenipotentiary makes specific mention of the island of Crete regarded important for Greek national defence and security. The importance of Crete to Greece was often compared to the strategic importance of Cuba to the U.S. at a time when U.S.-Mexican relations were at a nadir. See Sp. Markezinis, *Political History of Modern Greece*, Vol. 1, Athens: Papyros, 1966, p. 95, (in Greek).

by the Great Powers, which ratified the terms of the Constantinople Arrangement in connection with the border between Greece and the Ottoman Empire.

ARRANGEMENT* between Great Britain, France, Russia, and Turkey, for the Definitive Settlement of the Continental Limits of Greece. Signed at Constantinople, 21st July, 1832.

THE Representatives of the 3 Powers, parties to the Treaty of London, of the 6th of July, 1827, namely, the Right Honourable Sir Stratford Canning, Ambassador Extraordinary and Plenipoten-

---

* Ed. Hertslet, *The Map of Europe by Treaty*, Vol. III, London: Butterworths, 1875, pp. 903-908.

tiary of His Britannic Majesty, on a special mission to the Ottoman Sublime Porte; the Sieur Appolinaire Bouteneff, Envoy Extraordinary and Minister Plenipotentiary of His Majesty the Emperor of All the Russias; and the Sieur Jacques Edouard, Baron Burignot de Varenne, Chargé d' Affaires of His Majesty the King of the French, - having made known to the Sublime Ottoman Porte the changes which it was necessary to make in the Frontier of Greece, and having communicated to it the object of the instructions, and of the powers with which they were furnished, to propose to it a Definitive Boundary line, upon condition of compensating, by an equitable indemnity, the losses which might result therefrom: -the Sublime Porte, animated with the desire of consolidating the arrangements to which, out of consideration of the 3 Allied Courts, and relying on their sincere intentions, it had previously agreed, has consented to enter upon a negotiation for this purpose, and has charged therewith two of its Ministers, namely, His Excellency Mustapha Behdjet Effendi, Ex-Cazesker of Roumelia, at the present time First Physician of His Highness, and His Excellency Elhadj Mehemed Akif Effendi, present Reis Effendi.

The above-mentioned Plenipotentiaries, filled with the sentiments of their respective Governments, and having no other object in view than that of terminating the Greek Affair in a way that shall be durable, and calculated to prevent all further discussion on this question, have met several times for this salutary purpose; and the complete result of their conferences has been recorded in the present document, exchanged between the Parties as the instrument of their final transaction.

New Boundary.

It was agreed that:

ART.I. With respect to Boundary: On the eastern side, the extreme point of separation of the two States shall be fixed at the mouth of the little River which flows near the Village of Gradiza. The Frontier line shall ascend this River to its source, shall thence reach the chain of Mount Othryx, leaving to Greece the Passage of the Klomo, provided the crest of that chain be not passed: thence it shall follow, in a westerly direction, the crest of the same chain along the whole extent thereof, and especially the Peak of Vari-bovo, in order to attain the height which, under the denomination of Veluchi, forms the point of connection of the three great chains of mountains of the country. From this height the line shall continue, adapting itself as much as possible to the salient features of the country, across the Valley of the Aspropotamos to the Gulf of Arta, terminating at that Gulf between Coprina and Menidi, in such manner as that in any case the Bridge of Tartarina, the Defile and the Tower of Macrinoros shall be comprised within the Limits of Greece, and that the Bridge of Coracos and the Salt Springs of Coprina shall be left to the Ottoman Porte. Thus, the shore of the Gulf of Arta to the north and west of the point where the Boun-dary line meets its waters, will be retained by the Ottoman Empire; and the shore of this Gulf to the south and west of the line is assigned to the State of Greece, with the exception of the Fort of Punta, which will continue to belong to the Porte, with a radius of Territory which shall not be less than half-an-hour, nor more than an hour.

Nevertheless, as the Representatives, full of deference for the wish which has been expressed in the name of His Highness, relative to the portion of the district of Zeitoun, situate to the left of the Sperchius, have agreed that reference should be made on the subject to the Conference of London, upon the express condition that the decision and execution of the measures consequent thereupon should not be retarded thereby; it has become necessary to provide for the contingency of that portion of the Territory of Zeitoun remaining to the Ottoman Empire.

The Boundary line to the east will in that case commence at the mouth of the River Sperchius, and will run up its left Bank to the point of contact of the districts of Zeitoun and of Patradjik; thence it will reach the summit of the chain of the Othryx, following the common Boundary of those two districts, and the most direct line, in the event of that common Boundary not attaining the summit of the chain of the Othryx.

It will continue in the manner before mentioned, in order to terminate at the Gulf of Arta.

Indemnity to Turkey.

ART.II. With respect to the Indemnity, it remains fixed at the sum of 40,000,000 of Turkish piastres, provided the portions of the district of Zeitoun, situate to the left of the River Sperchius shall have been, in consequence of the decision of the Conference of London, definitively assigned to the Greek State.

If, on the other hand, in consequence of the decision of the Conference of London, those portions of the district of Zeitoun are to continue to belong to the Ottoman Empire, the indemnity which the Porte will receive remains fixed at the sum of 30,000,000 of Turkish piastres.

Appointment of Boundary Commissioners.

ART.III. The Commissioners of the 3 Courts shall immediately proceed to the marking out of the Boundary now settled. A Commissioner shall be appointed by the Sublime Porte to join in the labours of this Demarcation. It is clearly understood that no delay shall arise in this operation, whether from the absence of one or two of the Commissioners or from any other cause. A Commissioner appointed by the Greek Government may co-operate in the same labours, which should be completed in the space of 6 months, dating from this day. In case of difference of opinion

between the Commissioners, the question shall be equitably resolved by a majority of voices.[1]

Payment of Indemnity.

ART.IV. The Indemnity which is due to the Sublime Porte
in virtue of the present Arrangement, shall be paid on the 31st of
December of the present year, on which day, in conformity with
the following Article, all the Territories, without exception, which
are to constitute Greece shall be evacuated, if not sooner, by the
troops and authorities of the Sublime Porte. This payment shall
be effected at Constantinople on the 1st of December, 1832, at the
rate of exchange of the day of the signing of this instrument, by
drafts on London, Paris, Vienna, or Petersburgh; and the Porte
shall be officially informed on this matter on the arrival of the
formal confirmation of this transaction.

Turkish Evacuation of Greek Territories.

ART.V. On the 31st of December of the present year, or
sooner if possible, the Territories which form the object of the
present Arrangement shall be entirely evacuated by the Ottoman
troops and Authorities. With respect to the Territories previously
assigned to Greece, and which are still occupied by the Sublime
Porte, they also shall be evacuated within the same period, so that
on the day specified, the evacuation of all the Territories, without
exception, which are to constitute Greece, shall have been in every
instance completely effected.

---

1. The Commissioners were: for Great Britain, Lieut-Col.G. Baker; for
France, Lieut.-Col. J. Barthélemy; and for Russia, Col. A. Scalon.

Passage of Greek Vessels through the Gulf of Arta.

ART.VI. The Fort of Punta, as has been said above, being intended to remain to the Porte to complete the means of defence of Prevesa, and in order the better to secure the safety of its commerce, there shall only be permitted therein a garrison sufficient for the occupation of that post. It is understood that the Ottoman Authorities will not oppose any obstacle to the passage of Greek Vessels; and, excepting Customs dues and other imposts which would be due to the Sublime Porte in cases where Vessels may put into Punta, Prevesa, or other Turkish ports of the Gulf of Arta, the Authorities shall demand nothing for the passage.

*Permission to Individuals to quit Ceded Territories
and to sell their Estates.*

ART.VII. A term of 18 months, dating from the day on which the labours of the Demarcation shall have been completed, is accorded to such individuals as may desire to quit the Territories which form the object of the present Arrangement, and to sell their estates. This term of 18 months may, in special cases, and under unforeseen circumstances, be prolonged some months, and a Commission of Arbitration shall determine on the validity of these cases for exception, and shall assist in causing the sales to be effected at a fair price.

*Similar Privileges to Inhabitants of Eubea and Attica, and
Proprietors of Thebes.*

The same advantages are accorded to the inhabitants of the Island of Eubea, and of Attica, and to the Proprietors of Thebes, who would at the present day be in the receipt of their rightful revenues if that district were occupied by the Ottoman troops at the date of the assent of the Porte to the preceding arrangements of the 3rd of February, 1830.

It is understood that these individuals will alike be allowed to dispose, and within the same period, of any beneficial interest which they may have, either as tenants, or as hereditary administrators, in the *Vacoufs*, the whole of which is transferred to the Greek State.

Appointment of Commercial Agents.

ART.VIII. In conformity with the preceding stipulations, the Government of the new King of Greece will have the power of entering into negotiation for the purpose of regulating its relations of commerce and navigation with the Sublime Porte on a principle of reciprocity; and Agents duly accredited on either side shall be received in the Ports of Turkey and Greece, according to the usual forms, so that Ottoman subjects shall have an acknowledged right to traffic at their will in the State of Greece, and that, on their side, the Greeks shall cease to have recourse to foreign protection to frequent the Ports and Trading Towns of the Ottoman Empire.

Definitive Settlement of Greek Question.

The undersigned Plenipotentiaries of the 3 Courts, and those of the Sublime Porte, having brought to a close the Conferences which they have held for the purpose of effecting the Definitive Settlement of the Boundary of Greece, as above described, declare that, considering the arrangements recorded by common agreement in the present instrument, the object of the Treaty of London of the 6th July, 1827, and of the Protocols under different dates which relate thereto, is completely attained; that the prolonged negotiations to which those stipulations have given rise, are terminated in such a manner as never to be renewed; in fact, that the Greek Question is irrevocably settled.

Confirmation of Arrangement to have same force as a Ratification.

The final Confirmation of the present Final Arrangement by the 3 August Courts shall be transmitted to the Sublime Porte within the period of 4 months, dating from this day; and that Confirmation shall have, with respect to this Act, all the force of a Ratification.

Done at Constantinople, the 9th/21st July, 1832 (the 23rd of the month Safer, 1248 of the Hegira).

(L.S.) STRATFORD CANNING.

(L.S.) A. BOUTENEFF.

(L.S.) E.B. VARENNE.

TREATY OF LONDON

(29 March 1864)

THE TREATY *signed in London by the three Great Powers, Britain, France and Russia, on the one hand, and Greece on the other, ceded the Ionian Islands –which had never been conquered by the Ottomans– to the Kingdom of Greece. From the mid-fourteenth to the eighteenth century, the Ionian Islands had been under Venetian rule. When the sovereignty of Venice was overthrown by Napoleon (1797), the islands were recognised as independent (1800). The Paris Treaty of 1815 established the 'United States of the Ionian Islands' under British protection and the rule of a British High Commissioner.[1] Despite the Constitution granted to the Ionian Islands in 1817 and the reform law of 1823, social disturbances and conflict forced Britain to consider imposing martial law. At a Cabinet meeting on 8 December 1862,[2] under Foreign Secretary Palmerston, it was decided that the islands would be ceded to Greece – a policy favoured by Queen Victoria herself. There were three reasons for this decision. First, the islands had ceased to be of much significance to Britain since it could maintain its control of the seas from the much more strategic position of Malta. Second, the maintenance of British sovereignty in the area was proving too costly, and finally, Queen Victoria hoped that the cession of the islands would weaken Russia's hold on*

1.The islands were governed successively by the High Commissioners, Thomas Maitland, Sir Frederick Adam, Lord Ioannis Colbone-Baron of Seaton, Sir Henry George Ward, Sir Ioannis Young and Sir Henry Storks.

2. Earlier, in 1861, Lord Russell had offered the Ionian Islands to King Othon, on the condition that Greece would not engage in disputes with the Ottoman Empire at any time in the future. However, Othon had rejected Lord Russell's offer.

Greece by allowing the latter to realise one of its national aspirations at a negligible cost to Britain. Furthermore, the Danish Court had made the territorial expansion of Greece one of the conditions for George's acceptance of the Greek throne. The provisions of the treaty signed in London on 14 November 1863 were initially drawn up without Greek participation. After prolonged negotiations, however, the terms were altered to the satisfaction of Greece, before a new treaty was finally signed by Charilaos Trikoupis, the Greek delegate, on 29 March 1864. As a result, Greece now appeared as a High Contracting Party, whereas under the November 1863 Treaty, the Royal Councils of Europe had avoided entering into an agreement directly with the government of King George. Moreover, in the event of a war with the Ottoman Empire, the neutrality of the islands was only restricted to Corfu and Paxoi. In the absence of any new trade agreements, the privileges enjoyed by foreign nationals as well as commercial benefits would continue to apply for a period of ten years. The only contested provision of the 1863 text which was not altered, at the insistence of the French Emperor, was that concerning the protection of the privileges of the Latin Church.

The Ionian Islands were formally united with the Kingdom of Greece on 2 June 1864. This was the first expansion of the Greek kingdom since its foundation. The national territory increased by 1,813 square miles and the population by 236,000. However, the incorporation of the Ionian Islands to Greece also increased the economic burdens of the Greek state.

TREATY[*] between Great Britain, France, Russia, and Greece, respecting the Union of the Ionian Islands to the Kingdom of Greece. Signed at London, 29th March, 1864[1]

ART.   TABLE.

---

* Ed. Hertslet, *The Map of Europe by Treaty*, Vol. III, London: Butterworths, 1875, pp. 1589-1595.

1. The Sultan acceded to this Treaty on the 8th April, 1865.

Reference to Treaty of 5th November, 1815.

In the name of the Most Holy and Indivisible Trinity.

HER Majesty the Queen of the United Kingdom of Great Britain and Ireland made known to the Legislative Assembly of the United States of the Ionian Islands that, with a view to the eventual union of those Islands to the Kingdom of Greece, she was prepared, if the Ionian Parliament should express a wish to that effect, to abandon the Protectorate of those Islands, confided to Her Majesty by the Treaty concluded at Paris on the 5th November, 1815, between the Courts of Great Britain, Austria, Prussia, and Russia. Such wish having been expressed by a vote of the said Legislative Assembly passed unanimously on the 7/19th October, 1863, Her Britannic Majesty consented by Article I of the Treaty concluded on the 14th November, 1863, between Her Majesty, the Emperor of Austria, the Emperor of the French, the King of Prussia, and the Emperor of All the Russias, to renounce the said Protectorate under certain conditions specified in that Treaty, and since defined by subsequent Protocols.

On their part, their Majesties the Emperor of Austria, the Emperor of the French, the King of Prussia, and the Emperor of All the Russias, consented by the same Article, and under the same conditions, to accept such Renunciation, and to recognise, in conjunction with Her Britannic Majesty, the Union of those Islands to the Kingdom of Greece.

In virtue of Article V of the Treaty signed at London on the 13th July, 1863, it was moreover agreed by common consent between Her Britannic Majesty and their Majesties the Emperor of the French and the Emperor of All the Russias, that the Ionian Islands, when their Union to the Kingdom of Greece should have been effected, as contemplated by Article IV of the same Treaty, should be comprised in the Guarantee stipulated in favour of Greece by the Courts of Great Britain, France, and

Russia, in virtue of the Convention signed at London on the 7th May, 1832.

In consequence, and in accordance with the stipulations of the Treaty of the 13th July, 1863, and with the terms of Article VI of the Treaty of the 14th November, 1863, whereby the Courts of Great Britain, France, and Russia, in their character of Guaranteeing Powers of the Kingdom of Greece, reserved to themselves to conclude a Treaty with the Hellenic Government as to the arrangements which might become necessary in consequence of the Union of the Ionian Islands to Greece, their said Majesties have resolved to proceed to negotiate with His Majesty the King of the Hellenes a Treaty for the purpose of carrying into execution the stipulations above mentioned.

His Majesty the King of the Hellenes having given his assent to the conclusion of such Treaty, their said Majesties have named as their Plenipotentiaries, that is to say:

Her Majesty the Queen of the United Kingdom of Great Britain and Ireland, the Right Honourable John Earl Russell, Viscount Amberley of Amberley and Ardsalla, a Peer of the United Kingdom, a Member of Her Britannic Majesty's Privy Council, her Principal Secretary of State for Foreign Affairs; ·

His Majesty the Emperor of the French, the Sieur Godefroy Bernard Henry Alphonse, Prince de la Tour d' Auvergne Lauraguais, Ambassador Extraordinary and Plenipotentiary to Her Britannic Majesty, &c.;

His Majesty the Emperor of All the Russias, the Sieur Philip Baron de Brunnow, his Actual Privy Councillor, Ambassador Extraordinary and Plenipotentiary to Her Britannic Majesty, &c.;

And His Majesty the King of the Hellenes, the Sieur Charilaüs S.Tricoupi, a Representative in the National Assembly of the Hellenes;

Who, after having exchanged their Full Powers, found in good and due form, have agreed upon and signed the following Articles:

*Renunciation of Great Britain to Protectorate over the Ionian
Islands.*

ART. I. Her Majesty the Queen of the United Kingdom of
Great Britain and Ireland, desiring to realise the wish expressed
by the Legislative Assembly of the United States of the Ionian
Islands, that those Islands should be united to Greece, has
consented, on the conditions hereinafter specified, to renounce the
Protectorate over the Islands of Corfu, Cephalonia, Zante, Santa
Maura, Ithaca, Cerigo and Paxo, with their Dependencies, which,
in virtue of the Treaty signed at Paris on the 5th November, 1815,
by the Plenipotentiaries of Great Britain, Austria, Prussia, and
Russia, were constituted a single Free and Independent State,
under the denomination of «the United States of the Ionian
Islands» placed under the immediate and exclusive Protection of
His Majesty the King of the United Kingdom of Great Britain and
Ireland, his heirs and successors.

Union of Ionian Islands to Greece.

In consequence, Her Britannic Majesty, His Majesty the
Emperor of the French, and His Majesty the Emperor of All the
Russias, in their character of signing parties to the Convention
of the 7th May, 1832, recognise such Union, and declare that
Greece, within the Limits determined by the arrangement con-
cluded at Constantinople between the Courts of Great Britain,
France, and Russia, and the Ottoman Porte, on the 21st July,
1832, including the Ionian Islands, shall from [sic] a Monarchical,
Independent, and Constitutional State, under the Sovereignty of
His Majesty King George, and under the Guarantee of the 3
Courts.

Perpetual Neutrality of Ionian Islands.[2]

ART.II. The Courts of Great Britain, France, and Russia, in their character of Guaranteeing Powers of Greece, declare, with the assent of the Courts of Austria and Prussia, that the Islands of Corfu and Paxo, as well as their Dependencies, shall, after their Union to the Hellenic Kingdom, enjoy the advantages of perpetual Neutrality.

Greece to maintain the Neutrality.

His Majesty the King of the Hellenes engages, on his part, to maintain such Neutrality.

Treaties, &c., of Commerce and Navigation between Great Britain and Foreign Powers relative to Ionian Islands to remain in force until conclusion of New Treaty.[3]

ART.III. The Union of the Ionian Islands to the Hellenic Kingdom shall not involve any change as to the advantages conceded to Foreign Commerce and Navigation in virtue of Treaties and Conventions concluded by Foreign Powers with Her Britannic Majesty, in her character of Protector of the Ionian Islands.

All the engagements which result from the said transactions, as well as from the regulations actually in force in relation thereto, shall be maintained and strictly observed, as hitherto.

In consequence, it is expressly understood that Foreign

---

2. A Protocol on this Subject was also signed between the 5 Powers on the 25th January, 1864.

3. The Austrian and Prussian Governments assented to this Arrangement.

Vessels and Commerce in Ionian ports, as well as the Navigation between Ionian ports and the ports of Greece, shall continue to be subject to the same treatment, and placed under the same conditions as before the Union of the Ionian Islands to Greece, until the conclusion of new formal Conventions, or of arrangements destined to regulate between the parties concerned, questions of Commerce and Navigation, as well as questions relating to the regular service of communication by post.

Terms within which new Commercial Treaties are to be concluded.

Such new Conventions shall be concluded in 15 years, or sooner, if possible.[4]

Freedom of Worship and Religious Toleration.

ART.IV. The Union of the United States of the Ionian Islands to the Kingdom of Greece shall in no wise invalidate the principles established by the existing legislation of those Islands with regard to Freedom of Worship and Religious Toleration; accordingly the Rights and Immunities established in matters of Religion by Chapters I and V of the Constitutional Charter of the United States of the Ionian Islands, and specifically the recognition of the Orthodox Greek Church as the Dominant Religion in those Islands; the entire Liberty of Worship granted to the Established Church of the Protecting Power; and the perfect Toleration promised to other Christian communions shall, after the Union, be maintained in their full force and effect.

---

4. Ratified by the Sovereign of Great Britain on the 26th August, 1817.

The special Protection guaranteed to the Roman Catholic Church, as well as the advantages of which that Church is actually in possession, shall be equally maintained; and the subjects belonging to that communion shall enjoy in the Ionian Islands the same Freedom of Worship which is recognised in their favour by the Protocol of the 3rd February, 1830.

The principle of entire Civil and Political Equality between subjects belonging to different Creeds, established in Greece by the same Protocol, shall be likewise in force in the Ionian Islands.

Provision of Ionian Islands towards the Civil List of the King of the Hellenes.

ART.V. The Legislative Assembly of the United States of the Ionian Islands has decreed by a Resolution passed on the 7/19th October, 1863, that the sum of £10,000 sterling a year shall be appropriated, in monthly payments, to the augmentation of the Civil List of His Majesty the King of the Hellenes, so as to constitute the first charge upon the revenue of the Ionian Islands, unless provision be made for such payment, according to the constitutional forms, out of the revenues of the Kingdom of Greece.

In consequence, His Majesty the King of the Hellenes engages to carry that Decree duly into execution.

Relinquishment by Protecting Powers of portion of the Annual Sums to be paid to them by Greece.

ART.VI. Her Majesty the Queen of the United Kingdom of Great Britain and Ireland, His Majesty the Emperor of the French, and His Majesty the Emperor of All the Russias, agree to relinquish in favour of His Majesty King George I, each £4,000 sterling a year, out of the sums which the Greek Treasury has engaged to pay annually to each of them, in virtue of the arrangement concluded at Athens by the Greek Government, with the concurrence of the Greek Chambers, in the month of June, 1860.

Amounts relinquished to form Personal Dotation of King of Greece.

It is expressly understood that these 3 sums, forming a total of £12,000 sterling annually, shall be destined to constitute a Personal Dotation of His Majesty King George I, in addition to the Civil List fixed by the law of the State. The Accession of His Majesty to the Hellenic Throne shall not otherwise involve any change in the financial engagements which Greece has contracted by Article XII of the Convention of 7th May, 1832, towards the Powers Guarantees of the Loan, nor in the execution of the engagement taken by the Hellenic Government in the month of June, 1860, upon the representation of the 3 Courts.[5]

Contracts between Ionian Islands and Foreign Powers to be maintained by King of the Hellenes.

ART.VII. His Majesty the King of the Hellenes engages to take upon himself all the Engagements and Contracts lawfully concluded by the Government of the United States of the Ionian Islands, or in their name, by the Protecting Power of those Islands, conformably to the Constitution of the Ionian Islands, whether with Foreign Governments, with Companies and Associations, or with Private Individuals; and promises to fulfil the said

---

5. An Act of Parliament was passed on the 14th July, 1864 (27 and 28 Vict.,cap.40), to give effect to this Arrangement.

Engagements and Contracts fully and completely, as if they had been concluded by His Majesty or by the Hellenic Government. Under this head are specially included: the Public Debt of the Ionian Islands; the Privileges conceded to the Ionian Bank, to the Navigation Company known under the name of the Austrian Lloyds, in conformity with the Postal Convention of the 1st December, 1853, and to the Malta and Mediterranean Gas Company.

Pensions, &c., to British and Ionian Subjects to be Paid by Greece.

ART.VIII. His Majesty the King of the Hellenes promises to take upon himself,

1. The Pensions granted to British Subjects by the Ionian Government, in conformity with the rules established in the Ionian Islands respecting Pensions.

2. The Compensation Allowances due to certain individuals actually in the service of the Ionian Government, who will lose their employments in consequence of the Union of the Islands to Greece.

3. The Pensions which several Ionian Subjects are in the enjoyment of, in remuneration of services rendered to the Ionian Government.

Special Convention to regulate Amounts.

A Special Convention to be concluded between Her Britannic Majesty and His Majesty the King of the Hellenes shall determine the amounts of these different heads, and shall regulate the mode of their payment.

Withdrawal of British Forces from the Ionian Islands.

ART. IX. The Civil authorities and the Military Forces of Her Britannic Majesty shall be withdrawn from the Territory of the United States of the Ionian Islands in 3 months, or sooner, if possible, after the Ratification of the present Treaty.

Ratifications.[6]

ART.X. The present Treaty shall be ratified and the Ratifications shall be exchanged at London in 6 weeks, or sooner, if possible.

In witness whereof the respective Plenipotentiaries have signed the same, and have affixed thereto the Seal of their Arms. Done at London, the 29th of March, in the year of Our Lord, 1864.

(L.S.) RUSSELL.   (L.S.) CH.TRICOUPI.
(L.S.) LA TOUR D'AUVERGNE.
(L.S.) BRUNNOW.

---

6. Ratifications exchanged at London, 25th April, 1864.

CONVENTION OF CONSTANTINOPLE

(2 July 1881)

THE NEGOTIATIONS *leading to the signature of this convention took place in an unfavourable atmosphere for Greece, due to the opposition of the Ottoman Empire to the settlements of the Berlin Congress and its refusal to sign the thirteenth protocol (5 July 1878). This protocol which,* inter alia, *ceded Epirus to Greece, did not take account of the delicate manoeuvres which would be required in order to put that decision into effect and thus brought Greece and the Ottoman Empire, once more, to the threshold of war.[1] Faced with this danger and unable to impose their will on a still powerful Ottoman Empire,[2] the Great Powers chose to exert pressure on Greece, which in turn complied with the expediencies of international politics.[3] In a joint Note issued on 7 April 1881, the Powers called on the Greek government to accept the new border,[4] pledging to assist for a smooth transfer of power in the new territories and to protect the Christian populations, which would again come under Ottoman sovereignty.*

In the end, the Ottoman Empire and the Great Powers[5] signed a treaty on 24 May 1881 by which Thessaly, and what was later to become the Prefecture of Arta, were ceded to Greece. Greece, on its part, undertook, amongst other provisions, to respect the lives, honour, and

---

1. The Trikoupis government in Greece, declared a general mobilisation on 24 July 1880. The Porte retaliated by massing troops in Epirus and Thessaly.

2. France had already declared itself neutral, hoping to gain the support of Abdulhamit for its plan to take control over Tunisia.

3. It should be said, however, that Britain viewed acceptance of the Ottoman terms as a humiliation for Europe.

4. Arta-Volos line.

5. Germany, Austria, France, Britain, Italy and Russia.

property of the Muslims, and to allow them autonomy and their own religious courts.

Under Article 18 of the above treaty, its terms were to be reiterated, verbatim, in an agreement to be signed between the two states concerned. To this end, Greece and the Ottoman Empire signed the Convention in Constantinople on 2 July 1881. Representing signatories were Andreas Coundourioti,[6] Greek Ambassador in Constantinople, and Mahmoud Server Pasha, the Turkish Prime Minister.

The addition of new territories with an area of 13,395 square kilometres increased the population of Greece by 300,000 inhabitants, to a total of 2,187,208. This was the first time that territories from the Ottoman Empire were added to the modern Greek state since its foundation.

---

6. On the instructions of Koumoundouros government and with the consent of King George, who had returned from abroad after the fall of the Trikoupis government. However, the decision of the monarch and the government ran counter to popular sentiment.

Convention* avec la Grèce relative à la rectification des frontières Turco-Grecques.
Du 2 Juillet 1881.

— ᘛᘚ —

En exécution de l'Article XVIII de la Convention conclue le 24 Mai 1881 entre la Sublime Porte et les Représentants des Puissances co-signataires du Traité de Berlin, Leurs Majestés le Roi des Hellènes et l'Empereur des Ottomans étant convenus de conclure un acte reproduisant textuellement la dite Convention, ont désigné à cet effet:

Sa Majesté le Roi des Hellènes: le Sieur A.G. Coundourioti, Son Envoyé Extraordinaire et Ministre Plénipotentiaire près Sa Majesté l'Empereur des Ottomans,

Et Sa Majesté l' Empereur des Ottomans: Mahmoud Server Pacha, Président de Son Conseil d'Etat,

Lesquels, munis des pouvoirs nécessaires, ont arrêté ce qui suit:

ARTICLE I.

Les nouvelles frontières de la Turquie et de la Grèce sont fixées ainsi qu'il suit:

La nouvelle ligne frontière commençant près du défilé de Karanlik Dervend entre l'embouchure du Salamvrias et Platamona,

---

* Greek Ministry of Foreign Affairs, *Diplomatic Documents Addressing Frontier Issues*, Athens, 1882, pp. 293-299, (in Greek).

à quatre kilomètres environ au Sud de ce dernier point, se dirige vers l'Ouest en suivant la crête des montagnes, passe d'abord entre Krania et Avarnitza, puis entre Nézéros et Analypsis, arrive au sommet du Mont Godaman, descend ensuite vers le Sud en suivant la crête de l'Olympe, gange le sommet de Kokkinopetra et, prenant la direction de l'Ouest à partir de ce point sans quitter la même crête, passe entre Ligara et Derveni Melona et arrive au sommet du Mont Kritiri. Se dirigeant de là vers le Sud, la ligne atteint la rive droite de Xeraghis et, suivant la ligne de partage des eaux vers le Sud-Ouest, gagne le sommet des hauteurs situées au Nord du village de Zarko, tourne ensuite vers le Nord-Ouest dans la direction de Diminitza et se maintient toujours sur la ligne de partage des eaux en laissant à la Turquie le village d'Elevtherochorion. Avant d'arriver à Diminitza, à une distance d'environ 18 kilomètres de cette localité, la ligne frontière tourne vers l'Ouest toujours sur la ligne de partage des eaux et passe par les villages de Hamouristi, Gavranou et Georgitza pour gagner le sommet du Mont Kratchovo. Se dirigeant ensuite vers le Sud par la crête, elle passe par les sommets des Monts Zygos, Dokimi et Péristeri, et atteint la rivière d'Arta, en suivant le ruisseau qui conduit par la plus courte distance les eaux pluviales du sommet du Péristeri à ce cours d'eau et en passant près des villages de Kalarrhytes et de Michalitzi. Au delà de ces derniers points elle suit le thalweg de la rivière d'Arta jusqu'à son embouchure.

Cette délimitation sera fixée sur les lieux par une Commission composée des Délégués des six Puissances et des deux parties intéressées.

La Commission de délimitation prendra ses résolutions à la majorité des voix, chaque Puissance n'ayant qu'une voix.

Elle devra se réunir dans un délai de huit jours à partir de la ratification de la Convention du 24 mai dernier, ou plus tôt, si faire se peut, afin de commencer ses travaux.

ARTICLE II.

Punta et son territoire, tel qu'il a été déterminé par l' Art.I de l'acte signé à Constantinople le 21 juillet 1832, seront cédés à la Grèce. Toutes les fortifications qui commandent l'entrée du Golfe d'Arta, tant du côté de Prévésa que de celui de Punta, seront désarmées dans un délai de trois mois à partir de la signature de la Convention du 24 Mai dernier, et demeureront désarmées en temps de paix entre les deux Etats.

La navigation du Golfe d'Arta sera libre.

ARTICLE III.

La vie, les biens, l'honneur, la religion et les coutumes de ceux des habitants des localités cédées à la Grèce qui resteront sous l'administration hellénique seront scrupuleusement respectés. Ils jouiront entièrement des mêmes droits civils et politiques que les sujets hellènes d'origine.

ARTICLE IV.

Le droit de propriété sur les fermes ainsi que sur les pâturages, prairies, pacages (Kichlak), forêts et toute espèce de terrains ou autres immeubles possédés par des particuliers et des communes en vertu de firmans, hodjets, tapous et autres titres, ou bien de par la Loi Ottomane, dans les localités cédées à la Grèce, sera reconnu par le Gouvernement Hellénique. Les titres de propriété des biens dits vacoufs qui servent à l'entretien des mosquées, Collèges, Ecoles et autres établissements de piété ou de bienfaisance seront également reconnus.

A R T I C L E   V .

Sa Majesté le Sultan pourra disposer comme par le passé des propriétés Impériales, dont les revenus sont perçus pour le compte de Sa Majesté ou de la famille Impériale.

En cas de contestation sur la nature et la destination de ces biens, la question sera soumise à l'examen de la Commission, dont l'institution est prévue par l'Art.IX de la présente Convention, et éventuellement, aux termes du même Article, à la décision des Puissances Médiatrices.

A R T I C L E   V I .

Nul ne peut être privé de sa propriété que pour cause d'utilité publique dûment constatée dans les cas et de la manière établis par la Loi, moyennant une juste et préalable indemnité.

Aucun propriétaire ne pourra être forcé à vendre ses biens aux cultivateurs ou à des tiers, ni à leur en céder une partie, de même qu'aucune modification ne sera introduite dans les rapports des propriétaires et des cultivateurs, si ce n'est par une loi générale applicable à tout le Royaume.

Les propriétaires établis hors du Royaume et qui posséderaient des immeubles dans les territoires cédés, pourront affermer leurs immeubles ou les faire administrer par des tiers.

A R T I C L E   V I I .

Les habitants des provinces voisines des territoires cédés à la Grèce qui ont depuis longtemps la coutume d'envoyer leurs troupeaux dans les prairies et pâturages ainsi que dans les fermes situées sur ces territoires, continueront à jouir de ces avantages comme par le passé.

ARTICLE VIII.

La liberté ainsi que la pratique extérieure du culte sont assurées aux Musulmans dans les territoires cédés à la Grèce. Aucune atteinte ne sera portée à l'autonomie et à l'organisation hiérarchique des communautés musulmanes existantes ou qui pourraient se former, ni à l'administration des fonds et des immeubles qui leur appartiennent.

Aucune entrave ne pourra être apportée aux rapports de ces communautés avec leurs Chefs spirituels en matière de religion.

Les Tribunaux du Chéri locaux continueront à exercer leur juridiction en matière purement religieuse.

ARTICLE IX.

Une Commission Turco-hellénique sera chargée de régler, dans le courant de deux années, toutes les affaires concernant les propriétés de l'Etat ainsi que les questions relatives aux intérêts des particuliers, qui pourraient s'y trouver engagés. Cette Commission aura à statuer sur l'indemnité que la Grèce devra payer à la Turquie pour les biens fonds qui seraient reconnus appartenir *bona fide* à l'Etat Ottoman et lui donner un revenu annuel.

Les questions sur lesquelles une entente n'aura pas pu intervenir, seront soumises à la décision des Puissances Médiatrices.

ARTICLE X.

La Grèce devra supporter une part de la dette publique Ottomane proportionelle aux revenus des territoires cédés. Cette part sera déterminée ultérieurement entre la Sublime Porte et les Représentants des Puissances Médiatrices à Constantinople.

ARTICLE XI.

Aucune mesure exclusive et exceptionnelle de désarmement ne pourra être prise à l'égard des Musulmans.

ARTICLE XII.

Le Gouvernement hellénique présentera à la Chambre une Loi pour le renouvellement de la Convention de 1856 (1272) relative à la poursuite du bringandage.

ARTICLE XIII.

Les individus originaires des territoires cédés à la Grèce ou actuellement domiciliés dans ces provinces, qui entendront conserver la nationalité Ottomane, jouiront pendant l'espace de trois ans, à partir de l'échange des ratifications et moyennant une déclaration préalable faite à l'autorité compétente, de la faculté de transporter leur domicile dans l'Empire Ottoman et de s'y fixer, auquel cas la qualité de sujet Ottoman leur sera conservée.

Ceux qui émigreront dans le délai précité de trois ans continueront à jouir du bénéfice stipulé dans le troisième paragraphe de l'Art.VI de la présente Convention en faveur des propriétaires établis hors du Royaume.

Pendant le même espace de trois ans les Musulmans ne seront pas tenus au service militaire.

ARTICLE XIV.

La Commission créée en vertu de l' Article IX de la présente Convention est chargée de régler, dans le plus bref délai possible, les questions relatives aux impôts arriérés dans les territoires cédés qui seraient dûs au Gouvernement Ottoman, ainsi que celles qui pourraient surgir de la perception des impôts pendant l'année courante.

ARTICLE XV.

Les détails de l'évacuation ainsi que de la remise des territoires cédés sont réglés par un acte séparé, lequel est et demeure annexé à la présente Convention, et aura même force et valeur que s'il eñ faisait partie.

Les troupes Impériales Ottomanes seront tenues d' évacuer les territoires cédés dans les délais fixés par cet acte.

Le Gouvernement Impérial Ottoman s'efforcera toutefois de les abréger autant que possible.

ARTICLE XVI.

Il est entendu que les Puissances Médiatrices se réservent la faculté de déléguer des Commissaires techniques pour surveiller les opérations relatives à la cession des territoires.

ARTICLE XVII.

Une amnistie pleine et entière sera accordée par la Turquie et la Grèce à tous les individus qui auraient été impliqués ou compromis dans les événements politiques antérieurs à la présente Convention et relatifs à la question qu' elle résout.

ARTICLE XVIII.

La présente Convention sera ratifiée et les ratifications en seront échangées à Constantinople dans l'espace de trois semaines ou plus tôt si faire se peut.

En foi de quoi, les Plénipotentiaires respectifs l'ont signée et y ont apposé le sceau de leurs armes.

Fait à Constantinople, le deuxième jour du mois de Juillet (n.s.) de l'an mil huit cent quatre-vingt-un.

(L.S.) A.G. COUNDOURIOTI.
(L.S.) SERVER.

ANNEXE.

ARTICLE I.

Les territoires qui seront cédés à la Grèce sont divisés en six sections conformément aux indications marquées dans la Carte cî-annexée.

ARTICLE II.

L'évacuation d'une de ces sections aura lieu dans le terme de trois semaines à partir de la date fixée pour l'échange des Ratifications de la Convention, signée le 23 Mai dernier.

Quatre autres sections seront complétement évacuées dans l'espace de trois mois à partir de la même date.

La sixième section, qui comprend Volo et constitue le seul débouché par lequel le Gouvernement Ottoman puisse enlever son matériel, sera évacuée dans les deux mois suivants, c'est-à-dire, dans le délai total de cinq mois à partir de la date fixée pour l'échange des Ratifications de la même Convention. Il est entendu que ces différents délais seront abréges, si faire se peut.

Les Autorités Ottomanes dresseront l'inventaire de la partie du matériel qui ne pourrait être enlevée pendant le dit terme de cinq mois.

ARTICLE III.

Les Puissances Médiatrices nommeront des Délégués militaires qui constitueront une Commission appelée à servir d'intermédiaire pour l'évacuation par les Autorités Ottomanes, et la prise de possession par les Autorités Helléniques des territoires cédés.

Cette Commission exercera une surveillance générale sur l'évacuation ainsi que sur l'occupation des territoires cédés. Elle interviendra afin d'établir un accord entre les Commandants des deux parties, soit en ce qui concerne les mouvements militaires de part et d' autre, soit pour fixer la distance qui devra constamment séparer les troupes de deux Puissances, ainsi que le temps qui devra s'écouler entre l'évacuation et la prise de possession des différents points à céder.

ARTICLE IV.

Les Autorités Ottomanes et Grecques auront à donner aide et protection à cette Commission dans l'accomplissement de sa mission.

A R T I C L E   V .

Le présent acte fait partie intégrante de la Convention signée en ce jour à Constantinople et aura même force et valeur. En foi de quoi, les Plénipotentiaires respectifs l'ont signé et y ont opposé le cachet de leurs armes.

Fait à Constantinople, le deuxième jour du mois de Juillet (n.s.) de l'an mil huit cent quatre-vingt-un.

(L.S.) A.G. COUNDOURIOTI.

(L.S.) SERVER.

20TH CENTURY:

From the First Balkan War
to the Conclusion of the Second World War

LONDON PEACE TREATY

(30 May 1913)

THIS TREATY brought the First Balkan War to an end, though progress towards its signature was turbulent. An armistice was signed by the belligerents on 3 December 1912[1] while the peace conference opened two weeks later (16 December). Talks, however, soon broke down on 6 January 1913 as a result of the intransigent and provocative Ottoman stance. This stance, coupled with a new coup by the Young Turks in Constantinople (23 January 1913) caused hostilities to recommence (3 February 1913) and continue until the Ottoman Empire, weary and facing total disaster,[2] was compelled to sign the London Peace Treaty on 30 May 1913.

The proceedings of the Conference took place at St. James's Palace, where the treaty was also signed. The Greek delegation was headed by Prime Minister, Eleftherios Venizelos,[3] the Bulgarian by the Speaker of the Sobranje (Parliament), Dr S. Danoff, the Serbian by the former Prime Minister, L. Muskovic, the Montenegrian by Prime Minister, S. Novakovic, and that of the Ottoman Empire by Ahmed Rechid, Minister of Agriculture and Trade.

---

1. Greece alone among the belligerents deliberately chose not to be present at the signature of the armistice agreement, since after the Elli and Lemnos naval battles it had confined the Ottoman fleet to its base in the Dardanelles and completed its operations to occupy Epirus and the Aegean islands. This, however, did not prevent Greece from sending delegates to the peace conference a few days later.

2. Consecutive allied victories liberated the cities of Adrianople, Ioannina, Skutari, Tepeleni and Argyrokastro.

3. The delegation also included John Gennadius, Greek Ambassador in London, Professor N. Politis, and Lieutenant-General P. Danglis, Chief of the General Staff, with Captains I. Metaxas and A. Exadaktylos as his aides-de-camp.

*Despite considerable military accomplishments, especially at sea,
Greece was able to gain only such territories as its victories had secured.
Montenegro also felt wronged,[4] while Bulgaria received the most
favourable treatment of all.*

*The Treaty of London exacerbated the already strained relations
between Greece and Italy, since it was under Italian pressure that the
southern frontier of Albania was left undefined. Italy also continued to
ignore the demand of the people of the Dodecanese for union with Greece,
arguing instead that it was obliged to surrender the islands to the Sultan.*

*From the Greek point of view, the only positive outcome of the
negotiations and the resulting treaty was the delineation of the land
frontier of European Turkey (the Enos-Midia line) and the cession of
Crete to the Allies. The Great Powers assumed responsibility for the fate
of the Aegean Islands[5] and, as was the case with all the islands of the
Eastern Mediterranean basin, control over them was withdrawn from the
Porte. Finally, the Great Powers also assumed responsibility for the fate
of Mount Athos.*

*Although it was agreed on 30 May 1913, when the treaty was
signed,[6] that its terms were final, it ultimately came to be considered*

---

4. It was in the conference of ambassadors, being held simultaneously at
St. James's Palace, that the new frontiers in the Balkan peninsula were delineated.
The delegates to this parallel conference, chaired by the British Foreign Secretary,
Sir Edward Grey, were the ambassadors of the Great Powers in London. During
this conference, Montenegro was compelled to give up Skutari to the newly-
formed state of Albania.

5. See the Note of 13 February 1914 issued by the ambassadors of the
Great Powers to Greece. The Powers, which had assumed responsibility for the
islands through the London Peace Treaty, delayed reaching a final decision on the
islands' fate since, while they acknowledged the justice of the demand for their
incorporation into Greece, they also wished to use them as a lever to persuade
Greece to evacuate Northern Epirus.

6. The Treaty of London was never ratified, since the Second Balkan War,
caused largely by the Treaty itself and its terms, broke out a few weeks after its
signature. However, in a special protocol, the ambassadorial Conference of
Bucharest stated that it considered the treaty valid and that it empowered the
Conference to resolve the matters assigned to it. The treaty was published in the
Government Gazette (14 November 1913), but was never ratified by Royal

preliminary. Each ally was thus able to sign its own final treaty with the Ottoman Empire, settling in detail all the issues which had emerged from the war.

Decree. In legal terms, however, it is binding for Greece because it is referred to by the later Convention of Athens (Article 15), which was signed on 14 November 1913 and ratified by Law 4213 (Government Gazette 229/1913). See S.T. Laskaris, *The Diplomatic History of Greece, 1821-1914*, Athens, 1947, p. 241, note 1, (in Greek).

GRECE, BULGARIE, MONTENEGRO, SERBIE, TURQUIE.
Traité[*] de paix; signé à Londres, le 17/30 mai 1913.
Ephimeris du 14 novembre 1913.

———— ‿◦❀◦‿ ————

Sa Majesté le Roi des Hellènes, Sa Majesté le Roi des Bulgares, Sa Majesté le Roi de Monténégro et Sa Majesté le Roi de Serbie (ci-après désignés par les mots "les Souverains Alliés") d'une part,

et Sa Majesté l'Empereur des Ottomans d'autre part,

Animés du désir de mettre fin au présent état de guerre et de rétablir des relations de paix et d'amitié entre leurs Gouvernements et leurs sujets respectifs, ont résolu de conclure un Traité de Paix et ont choisi à cet effet pour leurs Plénipotentiaires:

Sa Majesté le Roi des Hellènes:

Son Excellence M. Etienne Skouloudis, ancien Ministre des Affaires Etrangères;

Son Excellence M. Jean Gennadius, Envoyé extraordinaire et Ministre plénipotentiaire à Londres;

Son Excellence M. Georges Streit, Envoyé extraordinaire et Ministre plénipotentiaire à Vienne.

Sa Majesté le Roi des Bulgares:

Son Excellence M. le Dr. Stoyan Danev, Président du Sobranié;

---

[*] H. Triepel, *Nouveau Recueil Général de Traités et autres actes relatifs aux rapports de droit international,* 3ème série, 8ème tome, Leipzig: Dieterich, 1914, pp. 16-19.

Son Excellence M. Michel Madjarov, Envoyé extraordinaire et Ministre plénipotentiaire à Londres.

Sa Majesté le Roi de Monténégro:

Son Excellence M. Jean Popovitch, ancien Chargé d'Affaires à Constantinople;

Son Excellence M. le Comte Louis Voïnovitch, ancien Ministre de la Justice.

Sa Majesté le Roi de Serbie:

Son Excellence M. Stoyan Novakovitch, ancien Président du Conseil des Ministres;

Son Excellence M. André Nikolitch, Président de la Skoupchtina;

Son Excellence M. Milenko Vesnitch, Envoyé extraordinaire et Ministre plénipotentiaire à Paris;

Son Excellence M. Jean Pavlovitch, ancien Ministre à Sophia.

Sa Majesté l'Empereur des Ottomans:

Son Excellence Osman Nizamy Pacha, Général de Division, ancien Ambassadeur à Berlin;

Son Excellence Batzaria Effendi, Sénateur, Ministre des Travaux publics;

Son Excellence Ahmed Réchid Bey, Conseiller-légiste de la Sublime Porte;

qui, après s'être communiqué leurs pleins pouvoirs et les avoir trouvés en bonne et due forme, sont convenus de ce qui suit:

ARTICLE 1.

Il y aura, à dater de l'échange des ratifications du présent traité, paix et amitié entre Sa Majesté l'Empereur des Ottomans d'une part, et Leurs Majestés les Souverains Alliés d'autre part, ainsi qu'entre Leurs héritiers et successeurs, Leurs Etats et sujets respectifs, à perpétuité.

ARTICLE 2.

Sa Majesté l'Empereur des Ottomans cède à Leurs Majestés les Souverains Alliés tous les territoires de son Empire sur le continent européen à l'ouest d'une ligne tirée d'Enos sur la mer Egée à Midia sur la mer Noire, à l'exception de l'Albanie.

Le tracé exact de la frontière d'Enos à Midia sera déterminé par une commission internationale.

ARTICLE 3.

Sa Majesté l'Empereur des Ottomans et Leurs Majestés les Souverains Alliés déclarent remettre à Sa Majesté l' Empereur d'Allemagne, à Sa Majesté l'Empereur d'Autriche, Roi de Bohême, &c., et Roi Apostolique de Hongrie, à M. le Président de la République Française, à Sa Majesté le Roi de Grande-Bretagne et d'Irlande et des Territoires britanniques au delà des Mers, Empereur des Indes, à Sa Majesté le Roi d'Italie et à Sa Majesté l'Empereur de toutes les Russies le soin de régler la délimitation des frontières de l'Albanie et toutes autres questions concernant l'Albanie.

ARTICLE 4.

Sa Majesté l'Empereur des Ottomans déclare céder à Leurs Majestés les Souverains Alliés l'île de Crète et renoncer en leur faveur à tous les droits de souveraineté et autres qu'il possédait sur cette île.

ARTICLE 5.

Sa Majesté l'Empereur des Ottomans et Leurs Majestés les

Souverains Alliés déclarent confier à Sa Majesté l'Empereur d'Allemagne, à Sa Majesté l'Empereur d'Autriche, Roi de Bohême, &c., et Roi Apostolique de Hongrie, à M. le Président de la République française, à Sa Majesté le Roi de Grande-Bretagne et d'Irlande et des Territoires britanniques au delà des Mers, Empereur des Indes, à Sa Majesté le Roi d'Italie et à Sa Majesté l'Empereur de toutes les Russies le soin de statuer sur le sort de toutes les îles ottomanes de la mer Egée, l'île de Crète exeptée, et de la péninsule du Mont-Athos.

ARTICLE 6.

Sa Majesté l'Empereur des Ottomans et Leurs Majestés les Souverains Alliés déclarent remettre le soin de régler les questions d'ordre financier résultant de l'état de guerre qui prend fin et des cessions territoriales ci-dessus mentionnées à la commission internationale convoquée à Paris, à laquelle ils ont délégué leurs représentants.

ARTICLE 7.

Les questions concernant les prisonniers de guerre, juridiction, nationalité et commerce seront réglées par des conventions spéciales.

ARTICLE FINAL.

Le présent traité sera ratifié et les ratifications seront échangées à Londres dans le plus bref délai possible.

En foi de quoi les Plénipotentiaires des Hautes Parties

contractantes ont signé le présent traité et y ont apposé leurs sceaux.

Fait à Londres, le 17 (30) mai 1913, à midi (heure de Greenwich).

Etienne Skouloudis.
J. Gennadius.
G. Streit.

Dr. St. Daneff.
M. Iv. Madjaroff.

J. Popovitch.
L. de Voïnovitch.

Stojan Novakovitch.
And. Nikolitch.
Mil. R. Vesnitch.
Ivan Pavlovitch.

Osman Nizamy.
N. Batzaria.
Ahmed Réchid.

PEACE TREATY OF BUCHAREST

(10 August 1913)

To the relatively brief text of this treaty were appended three proto-cols concerning the frontiers of Bulgaria, which had been defeated in the Second Balkan War. The third of these protocols referred to Greece, which at the end of the War had acquired Crete[1] and Kavala. The northern frontier of Greece was defined as extending from the north of Korytsa, between Monastir and Florina, to Doiran, then south of Strumitsa, Petrich and Nevrokopi, to the mouth of the Nestos (Mesta).

The Peace Treaty of Bucharest was the outcome of the conference convened after the conclusion of the Second Balkan War, on the initiative of King Carol of Roumania.[2] Bulgaria lost the greater part of Macedonia, whose territory was divided between Greece and Serbia. During the conference, the Bulgarian delegates at times adopted an attitude that was seen as provocative by the other participants, given that Bulgaria had been the aggressor and was, moreover, the defeated side. There were also times, however, when they were strikingly conciliatory. This was because Bulgaria hoped that the Great Powers would revise the treaty, a hope encouraged by both Austria and Russia. France and Germany were opposed to such a revision, while Italy and Britain were prepared to accept it only if it was unanimously agreed upon. The European Powers were wary of the possibility of further unrest in the Balkans.

The delegations were headed at the conference by their respective Prime Ministers; Greece was represented by Eleftherios Venizelos, Serbia

---

1. Serbia waived all its claims on Crete under the Pachic-Venizelos Minute of 16 August 1913.

2. Roumania declared war on Bulgaria in July 1913 and its troops were closing in on the Bulgarian capital.

by N. Pachic, Roumania by T. Maioresco and Montenegro by S. Vou-kotic, whilst defeated Bulgaria was represented by Finance Minister D. Tontchev.

Through the Treaty of Bucharest, the territory of Greece doubled in size[3] and its population increased by some two million, reaching 4,718,221 inhabitants.[4] Although this expansion could have been considerably greater, it was significant as it included sources of wealth, providing the conditions for industrialisation and economic development. It also improved Greece's international standing. With its special position in the network of Balkan relations and in the balance of political and military power in Europe, the modern Greek state acquired an unprecedented role.

---

3. From 63,211 to 120,308 square kilometres.

4. After the Treaty, the populations of the other Balkan countries were approximately as follows: Serbia 4,000,000, Roumania 7,000,000, and Bulgaria 5,000,000. In August 1913, Greece was compelled - for reasons connected with Great Power political expediency - to withdraw its troops from the parts of Western Thrace which it had occupied. As a result, a considerable number of Greeks had to emigrate.

ROUMANIE , GRECE , MONTENEGRO, SERBIE, BULGARIE.

Traité* de paix; signé à Bucarest, le 28 juillet / 10 août 1913,
suivi de deux Procès - verbaux d'échange des ratifications.
Publication officielle. Bucarest 1913.

— ◄●► —

TRAITE DE PAIX

Leurs Majestés le Roi de Roumanie, le Roi des Hellènes, le Roi de Monténégro et le Roi de Serbie, d'une part, et Sa Majesté le Roi des Bulgares, d'autre part, animés du désir de mettre fin à l'état de guerre actuellement existant entre Leurs pays respectifs, voulant, dans une pensée d'ordre, établir la paix entre Leurs peuples si longtemps éprouvés, ont résolu de conclure un Traité définitif de paix. Leurs dites Majestés ont, en conséquence, nommé pour Leurs Plénipotentiaires, savoir:

Sa Majesté le Roi de Roumanie :

Son Excellence Monsieur Titus Maïoresco, Son Président du Conseil des Ministres, Ministre des Affaires Etrangères;

Son Excellence Monsieur Alexandre Marghiloman, Son Ministre des Finances;

Son Excellence Monsieur Take Ionesco, Son Ministre de l'Intérieur;

---

* H. Triepel, *Nouveau Recueil Général de Traités et autres actes relatifs aux rapports de droit international*, 3ème série, 8ème tome, Leipzig: Dieterich, 1914, pp. 61-65.

Son Excellence Monsieur Constantin G. Dissesco, Son Ministre des Cultes et de l'Instruction Publique;
Le Général de division aide de camp C. Coanda, Inspecteur général de l'artillerie, et
Le Colonel C. Christesco, Sous-chef du grand état-major de Son armée.

Sa Majesté le Roi des Hellènes:
Son Excellence Monsieur Eleftéris Veniselos, Son Président du Conseil des Ministres, Ministre de la Guerre;
Son Excellence Monsieur Démètre Panas, Ministre Plénipotentiaire;
Monsieur Nicolas Politis, Professeur de droit international à l'Université de Paris;
Le Capitaine Ath. Exadactylos, et
Le Capitaine C. Pali.

Sa Majesté le Roi de Monténégro:
Son Excellence le Général Serdar Yanko Voukotitch, Son Président du Conseil des Ministres, Ministre de la Guerre, et
Monsieur Jean Matanovitch, Ancien Chargé d' Affaires de Monténégro à Constantinople.

Sa Majesté le Roi de Serbie:
Son Excellence Monsieur Nicolas P. Pachitch, Son Président du Conseil des Ministres, Ministre des Affaires Etrangères;
Son Excellence Monsieur Mihaïlo G. Ristitch, Son Envoyé Extraordinaire et Ministre Plénipotentiaire à Bucarest;
Son Excellence Monsieur le Docteur Miroslaw Spalaïkovitch, Envoyé Extraordinaire et Ministre Plénipotentiaire;
Le Colonel K. Smilianitch, et
Le Lieutenant Colonel D. Kalafatovitch.

Sa Majesté le Roi des Bulgares:
Son Excellence Monsieur Dimitri Tontcheff, Son Ministre des Finances;
Le Général-Major Ivan Fitcheff, Chef de l'état-major de Son armée;

Monsieur Sawa Ivantchoff, docteur en droit, ancien Vice-Président du Sobranié;

Monsieur Siméon Radeff, et

Le Lieutenant Colonel d'état-major Constantin Stancioff.

Lesquels, suivant la proposition du Governement Royal de Roumanie, se sont rénuis en Conférence à Bucarest, munis de pleins pouvoirs, qui ont été trouvés en bonne et due forme.

L'accord s'étant heureusement établi entre eux, ils sont convenus des stipulations suivantes:

ARTICLE PREMIER.

Il y aura, à dater du jour de l'échange des ratifications du présent Traité, paix et amitié entre Sa Majesté le Roi de Roumanie, Sa Majesté le Roi des Hellènes, Sa Majesté le Roi de Monténégro, Sa Majesté le Roi de Serbie et Sa Majesté le Roi des Bulgares, ainsi qu'entre Leurs héritiers et successeurs, Leurs Etats et sujets respectifs.

ARTICLE II.

Entre le Royaume de Bulgarie et le Royaume de Roumanie, l'ancienne frontière entre le Danube et la Mer Noire est, conformément au procès-verbal arrêté par les Délégués militaires respectifs et annexé au Protocole No 5 du 22 juillet (4 août) 1913 de la Conférence de Bucarest, rectifiée de la manière suivante:

La nouvelle frontière partira du Danube, en amont de Turtukaïa, pour aboutir à la Mer Noire au Sud d'Ekrene.

Entre ces deux points extrêmes, la ligne frontière suivra le tracé indiqué sur les cartes 1/100.000 et 1/200.000 de l'état-major roumain, et selon la description annexées au présent article.

Il est formellement entendu que la Bulgarie démantélera, au

plus tard dans un délai de deux années, les ouvrages de fortifications existants et n'en construira pas d'autres à Roustchouk, à
Schoumla, dans le pays intermédiaire, et dans une zône de vingt
kilomètres autour de Baltchik.

Une commission mixte, composée de représentants des
deux Hautes Parties contractantes, en nombre égal des deux côtés,
sera chargée, dans les quinze jours qui suivront la signature du
présent Traité, d'exécuter sur le terrain le tracé de la nouvelle
frontière, conformément aux stipulations précédentes. Cette
commission présidera au partage des biens-fonds et capitaux qui
ont pu jusqu'ici appartenir en commun à des districts, des communes, ou des communautés d'habitants séparés par la nouvelle
frontière. En cas de désaccord sur le tracé et les mesures d'exécution, les deux Hautes Parties contractantes s'engagent à s'adresser
à un Gouvernement tiers ami pour le prier de désigner un arbitre
dont la décision sur les points en litige sera considérée comme
définitive.

ARTICLE III.

Entre le Royaume de Bulgarie et le Royaume de Serbie, la
frontière suivra, conformément au procès-verbal arrêté par les
Délégués militaires respectifs et annexé au Protocole No 9 du 25
juillet (7 août) 1913 de la Conférence de Bucarest, le tracé suivant:
La ligne frontière partira de l'ancienne frontière du sommet
Patarica, suivra l'ancienne frontière turco-bulgare et la ligne de
partage des eaux entre le Vardar et la Strouma avec l'exception
que la haute vallée de la Stroumitza restera sur territoire serbe; elle
aboutira à la montagne Belasica, où elle se reliera à la frontière
bulgaro-grecque. Une description détaillée de cette frontière et son
tracé sur la carte 1/200.000 de l'état-major autrichien, sont annexés
au présent article.

Une commission mixte, composée de représentants des

deux Hautes Parties contractantes, en nombre égal des deux côtés sera chargée, dans les quinze jours qui suivront la signature du présent Traité, d'exécuter sur le terrain le tracé de la nouvelle frontière, conformément aux stipulations précédentes.

Cette commission présidera au partage des biens-fonds et capitaux qui ont pu jusqu'ici appartenir en commun à des districts, des communes, ou des communautés d'habitants séparés par la nouvelle frontière. En cas de désaccord sur le tracé et les mesures d'exécution, les deux Hautes Parties contractantes s'engagent à s'adresser à un Gouvernement tiers ami pour le prier de désigner un arbitre dont la décision sur les points en litige sera considérée comme définitive.

ARTICLE IV.

Les questions relatives à l'ancienne frontière serbo-bulgare seront réglées suivant l'entente intervenue entre les deux Hautes Parties contractantes, constatée dans le Protocole annexé au présent article.

ARTICLE V.

Entre le Royaume de Grèce et le Royaume de Bulgarie, la frontière suivra, conformément au procès-verbal arrêté par les Délégués militaires respectifs et annexé au Protocole No 9 du 25 juillet (7 août) 1913 de la Conférence de Bucarest, le tracé suivant:

La ligne frontière partira de la nouvelle frontière bulgaro-serbe sur la crête de Belasica planina, pour aboutir à l'embouchure de la Mesta à la Mer Egée.

Entre ces deux points extrêmes, la ligne frontière suivra le tracé indiqué sur la carte 1/200.000 de l'état-major autrichien et selon la description annexées au présent article.

Une commission mixte, composée de représentants des deux Hautes Parties contractantes, en nombre égal des deux côtés, sera chargée, dans les quinze jours qui suivront la signature du présent Traité, d'exécuter sur le terrain le tracé de la frontière conformément aux stipulations précédentes.

Cette commission présidera au partage des biens-fonds et capitaux qui ont pu jusqu'ici appartenir en commun à des districts, des communes, ou des communautés d'habitants séparés par la nouvelle frontière. En cas de désaccord sur le tracé et les mesures d'exécution, les deux Hautes Parties contractantes s'engagent à s'adresser à un Gouvernment tiers ami pour le prier de désigner un arbitre dont la décision sur les points en litige sera considérée comme définitive.

Il est formellement entendu que la Bulgarie se désiste, dès maintenant, de toute prétention sur l'île de Crète.

ARTICLE VI.

Les Quartiers généraux des armées respectives seront aussitôt informés de la signature du présent Traité. Le Gouvernement bulgare s'engage à ramener son armée, dès le lendemain de cette signification, sur le pied de paix. Il dirigera les troupes sur leurs garnisons où l'on procédera, dans le plus bref délai, au renvoi des diverses réserves dans leurs foyers.

Les troupes dont la garnison se trouve située dans la zône d'occupation de l'armée de l'une des Hautes Parties contractantes, seront dirigées sur un autre point de l'ancien territoire bulgare et ne pourront gagner leurs garnisons habituelles qu' après évacuation de la zône d'occupation sus-visée.

ARTICLE VII.

L'évacuation du territoire bulgare, tant ancien que nouveau, commencera aussitôt après la démobilisation de l'armée bulgare, et sera achevée au plus tard dans la quinzaine. Durant ce délai, pour l'armée d'occupation roumaine, la zône de démarcation sera indiquée par la ligne Sistov-Lovcea-Turski-Izvor-Glozene-Zlatitza-Mirkovo-Araba-Konak-Orchania-Mezdra-Vratza-Berkovitza-Lom-Danube.

ARTICLE VIII.

Durant l'occupation des territoires bulgares les différentes armées conserveront le droit de réquisition, moyennant paiement en espèces.

Elles y auront le libre usage des lignes de chemin de fer pour les transports de troupes et les approvisionnements de toute nature, sans qu' il y ait lieu à indemnité au profit de l'autorité locale.

Les malades et les blessés y seront sous la sauvegarde des dites armées.

ARTICLE IX.

Aussitôt que possible après l'échange des ratifications du présent Traité, tous les prisonniers de guerre seront réciproquement rendus.

Les Gouvernements des Hautes Parties contractantes désigneront chacun des Commissaires spéciaux chargés de recevoir les prisonniers.

Tous les prisonniers aux mains d'un des Gouvernements seront livrés au commissaire du Gouvernement auquel ils appartiennent ou à son représentant dûment autorisé, à l'endroit qui sera fixé par les parties intéressées.

Les Gouvernements des Hautes Parties contractantes présenteront respectivement l'un à l'autre, et aussitôt que possible après la remise de tous les prisonniers, un état des dépenses directes supportées par lui pour le soin et l'entretien des prisonniers, depuis la date de la capture ou de la reddition jusqu'à celle de la mort ou de la remise. Compensation sera faite entre les sommes dues par la Bulgarie à l'une des autres Hautes Parties contractantes et celles dues, et la différence sera payée au Gouvernement créancier aussitôt que possible après l'échange des états de dépenses sus-visés.

ARTICLE X.

Le présent Traité sera ratifié et les ratifications en seront échangées à Bucarest dans le délai de quinze jours ou plus tôt si faire se peut.

En foi de quoi, les Plénipotentiaires respectifs l'ont signé et y ont apposé leurs sceaux.

Fait à Bucarest le vingt huitième jour du mois de juillet (dixième jour du mois d'août) de l'an mil neuf cent treize.

Signés:

Pour la Roumanie: Pour la Bulgarie:

(L.S.) T. Maïoresco   (L.S.) D. Tontcheff
Al. Marghiloman   Général Fitcheff
Take Ionesco   Dr. S. Ivantchoff
C.G. Dissesco   S. Radeff
Général aide de camp Coanda   Lt Colonel Stancioff
Colonel C. Christesco

Pour la Grèce:

(L.S.) E.K. Veniselos
D. Panas
N. Politis
Capitaine A. Exadactylos
Capitaine C. Pali

Pour le Monténégro:

(L.S.) Général Serdar I. Voukotitch
Y. Matanovitch

Pour la Serbie:

(L.S.) Nik. P. Pachitch
M. G. Ristitch
M. Spalaïkovitch
Colonel K. Smilianitch
Lt Colonel D. Kalafatovitch

PEACE CONVENTION OF ATHENS

(14 November 1913)

The PEACE CONVENTION *signed in Athens between Greece and the Ottoman Empire finally restored peaceful relations between the two countries which had been at war for two years. The Convention dealt chiefly with the nationality of those living in the new Greek provinces and the protection of the religious privileges of the Muslims residing there. In effect, by signing this bilateral convention, Greece and the Ottoman Empire stated their commitment to respect the terms of the Treaty of London (30 May 1913). However, the main issue still outstanding was the status of the Aegean islands: the Ottoman Empire did everything in its power to prevent them from being awarded to Greece, while the Greek government insisted on their incorporation to the Greek state. The Great Powers, on the other hand, were content with the matter remaining in abeyance until the southern borders of Albania were finally settled, since it provided them with a means of exerting pressure on Athens to accept without protest the cession of Northern Epirus to Albania.*

Convention* de Paix d' Athènes

PREAMBULE

Sa Majesté le Roi des Hellènes et Sa Majesté l'Empereur des Ottomans, animés d'un égal désir de consolider les liens de paix et d'amitié heureusement rétablis entre Eux et de faciliter la reprise des relations normales entre les deux pays, ont résolu de conclure une Convention à cet effet, et ont nommé pour leurs Plénipotentiaires, savoir:
Sa Majesté le Roi des Hellènes Son Excellence Monsieur D. Pamas, Ministre des Affaires Etrangères, et Sa Majesté l'Empereur des Ottomans Son Excellence Ghalib Kémaly Bey, Plénipotentiaire Ottoman,
Lesquels, après s'être communiqué leurs pleins pouvoirs trouvés en bonne et due forme, sont convenus de ce qui suit:
[...]

ARTICLE 15.

Les deux Hautes Parties contractantes s'engagent à maintenir, en ce qui les concerne, les dispositions du Traité de Londres du 30 mai 1913, y compris les stipulations de l'article 5 du dit Traité.

---

* Greek Government Gazette, No 229, Issue A, 14 November 1913, pp. 813-816.

ARTICLE 16.

Le présent Traité entrera en vigueur immédiatement après sa signature.

Les ratifications en seront échangées dans la quinzaine à dater de ce jour.

En foi de quoi les Plénipotentiaires respectifs l'ont signé et ont apposé leurs cachets.

Fait en double exemplaire à Athènes 1/14 Novembre 1913.

(L.S.) D. PANAS   (L.S.) GHALIB KEMAL.

NOTE OF THE GREAT POWERS TO GREECE

(13 February 1914)

THE NOTE was delivered to the Greek government by the ambassadors of the Great Powers in Athens. It concerned the decision of the Powers to cede irrevocably to Greece all the Aegean islands already occupied by the latter (with the exception of Imbros, Tenedos and Castellorizo) on the date on which Greek troops would evacuate the parts of Northern Epirus awarded to Albania by the Florence Protocol of 17 December 1913.[1] Three days later (16 February 1914), the Ottoman Empire replied to the Note, agreeing to undertake and to be responsible for this specific initiative. Five days later (21 February 1914), Greece too, replied, stating its satisfaction that the question of the sovereignty of the Aegean islands had been resolved.

Venizelos, eager to reach a favourable settlement on at least one of the two questions still outstanding for Greece, had no alternative but to accept Sir Edward Grey's proposal to the first ambassadorial Conference in London; i.e., to withdraw Greek troops from Northern Epirus[2] as a condition for the handing over of the Aegean islands to Greece.[3] However, Venizelos proposed rectifications to the Greek-Albanian

---

1. This was a text prepared by the commission which drew the Greek-Albanian border. The new line ran SW-NW from Ftelia to Lake Prespa, at a distance of about 40 km from Ioannina. Albania was also awarded the Argyrokastro valley and the towns of Argyrokastro, Lekoviski, Delvino, Aghioi Saranta, Tepeleni, Premeti and Korytsa.

2. The majority of the inhabitants in the area claimed by Greece (Northern Epirus) were Greek-speaking, or Albanian-speaking with a Greek national consciousness.

3. In reply to the Ottoman demand that the islands should not be fortified, Venizelos demanded that the Great Powers guarantee their neutrality and security (February 1914).

border near Korytsa and asked for guarantees of the religious, educational and property rights of the Greeks of Northern Epirus.

When the Greek troops withdrew, the guerrilla war in Northern Epirus escalated.[4] Britain and Russia proposed a delay in the complete evacuation of the area by Greek troops, and the formation of an international corps to maintain order. The situation deteriorated, however, as the European Powers delayed in making a decision. In an attempt to stop the bloodshed, the international control commission in Albania decided to negotiate with representatives of the autonomists. An agreement was finally reached (Corfu, 17 May 1914) on an arrangement under which the Epirots of the disputed areas would enjoy considerable autonomy. However, none of the Great Powers seemed prepared to guarantee the implementation of the Corfu agreement, especially after the breakout of the First World War which led to anarchy, diminishing any probability of peace in the region.

---

4. On 17 February 1914, after the withdrawal of the Greek troops, Northern Epirus declared itself autonomous under the interim presidency of Georgios Christakis-Zographos, who had previously been General Commander of Epirus.

Note[*] des représentants d' Allemagne, d' Autriche-Hongrie, de Grande-Bretagne, d' Italie et de Russie au Gouvernement Grec, en date du 31 Janvier/13 Février 1914.

D' après l' article 5 du traité de Londres, en date du 17/30 Mai 1913 entre la Turquie et les Etats alliés balkaniques, ainsi qu' aux termes de l' article 15 du traité signé à Athènes entre la Grèce et la Turquie le 1er Novembre 1913, le gouvernement grec s' est engagé à laisser aux six puissances le soin de décider du sort des îles de la mer Egée.

En conséquence les six puissances ont décidé de remettre à la Grèce toutes les îles de la mer Egée actuellement occupées par elle, à l' exception de Tenedos, d' Imbros et de Castellorizo, qui doivent être restituées à la Turquie.

Les puissances ont décidé en outre, en ce qui concerne les îles assignées à la Grèce, que des garanties satisfaisantes devront leur être données, ainsi qu' à la Turquie, par le gouvernement grec: que ces îles ne seront ni fortifiées ni utilisées pour aucun but naval ou militaire et que des mesures effectives seront prises pour prévenir la contrebande entre les îles et le continent ottoman.

Les six puissances se sont engagées à user de leur influence sur le gouvernement grec en vue d' assurer l' exécution loyale et le maintien de ces conditions. Elles demandent en outre à la Grèce de donner des garanties satisfaisantes au sujet de la protection des

* Ch. Strupp, *La Situation Internationale de la Grèce 1821-1917*, Zürich: Die Verbinbung, pp. 232-233.

minorités musulmanes dans les îles qu' elle acquiert, en vertu de la décision des six puissances mentionnées ci-dessus.

L' attribution définitive à la Grèce des îles que les six puissances décident de laisser en sa possession ne deviendra effective que lorsque les troupes grecques auront évacué les territoires assignés à l' Albanie, en vertu du protocole de Florence en date du 17 décembre 1913 ci-annexé, de même que l' île de Saseno, et lorsque le gouvernement grec se sera formellement engagé à n' opposer aucune résistance et à ne soutenir ni à encourager directement ni indirectement aucune résistance d' aucun genre à l' état des choses établi par les puissances dans l' Albanie du sud.

L' évacuation commencera le 1er mars (nouveau style), par le retrait des troupes grecques du Caza de Korytza et de l' île Saseno, et procédera successivement, jusqu' au 31 mars (nouveau style), date à laquelle elle devra prendre fin par le départ des troupes helléniques du Caza de Delvino.

Les six puissances ont confiance que les décisions ci-dessus seront loyalement respectées par le gouvernement grec.

QUADT.   SZILASSY.   DEVILLE.
ELLIOT.   BOSDARI.   DEMIDOF.

TREATY OF NEUILLY

(27 November 1919)

THE NEUILLY TREATY was the third peace treaty to be signed after the end of the First World War. It concerned Bulgaria, the first of the Central Powers forced to capitulate. However, it was also of particular interest to Greece, since it restored to Greek sovereignty the areas of Macedonia invaded during the War by German and Bulgarian troops.

Delegates from 21 countries - apart from Bulgaria - attended the conference, in the Town Hall of Neuilly-sur-Seine, a suburb of Paris. The Greek delegation, headed by Venizelos, submitted a stern and closely-argued memorandum in support of the Greek claims.

The conference decided that:
- Greece would recover the territory in Macedonia which belonged to it before the War
- Bulgaria would renounce all claims in Western Thrace [1, 2]
- Bulgaria would be compelled to pay reparations
- The size of the Bulgarian Army would be reduced
- The minorities on Bulgarian soil - including the Greek minority - would be protected (a convention on mutual and voluntary migration was also signed)
- Bulgaria would be obliged to return cultural artefacts of archaeological, historical and artistic value which had been

---

1. The Bulgarian renunciation of its rights in Western Thrace, in favour of Greece, was confirmed by the Treaty of Sèvres (1920).

2. By the Paris Peace Treaty of 10 February 1947, Bulgaria returned to the borders of 1 January 1941 - that is, as set by the Treaty of Neuilly. It thus abandoned all its claims over northern Greece, while retaining south Dobrudja.

looted from the country during the period when Bulgarian troops were present in Greece.

The Neuilly Treaty contained 296 relatively brief articles and a large number of appendices. It was undoubtedly of great significance for Greece, since Bulgaria, its greatest adversary in the Balkans, was stripped of a great part of its strength and the conditions were created for the cession, at a later date, of part or the whole of Eastern Thrace to Greece.

TREATY* OF NEUILLY

The United States of America, the British Empire, France, Italy and Japan,

These Powers being described in the present Treaty as the Principal Allied and Associated Powers;

Belgium, China, Cuba, Greece, the Hedjaz, Poland, Portugal, Roumania, the Serb-Croat-Slovene State, Siam and Czecho-Slovakia,

These Powers constituting, with the Principal Powers mentioned above, the Allied and Associated Powers,

of the one part;

And Bulgaria,

of the other part;

Whereas on the request of the Royal Government of Bulgaria an Armistice was granted to Bulgaria on September 29, 1918, by the Principal Allied and Associated Powers in order that a Treaty of Peace might be concluded, and

Whereas the Allied and Associated Powers are equally de-

---

* *The Treaties of Peace : 1919-1923*, Vol. II, New York : Carnegie Endowment Ed., 1924, pp. 651-785.

sirous that the war in which certain among them were successively involved, directly or indirectly, against Bulgaria, and which originated in the declaration of war against Serbia on July 28, 1914, by Austria-Hungary, and in the hostilities opened by Bulgaria against Serbia on October 11, 1915, and conducted by Germany in alliance with Austria-Hungary, with Turkey and with Bulgaria, should be replaced by a firm, just and durable Peace,

For this purpose the High Contracting Parties have appointed as their Plenipotentiaries:

The President of the United States of America:
The Honourable Frank Lyon Polk, Under-Secretary of State;
The Honourable Henry White, formerly Ambassador Extraordinary and Plenipotentiary of the United States at Rome and Paris;
General Tasker H.Bliss, Military Representative of the United States on the Supreme War Council;

His Majesty the King of the United Kingdom of Great Britain and Ireland and of the British Dominions beyond the Seas, Emperor of India:
Mr. Cecil Harmsworth, M.P., Under-Secretary of State for Foreign Affairs;
Sir Eyre Crowe, K.C.B., K.C.M.G., Minister Plenipotentiary, Assistant Under-Secretary of State for Foreign Affairs;
And
for the Dominion of Canada:
The Honourable Sir George Halsey Perley, K.C.M.G., High Commissioner for Canada in the United Kingdom;

for the Commonwealth of Australia:
The Right Honourable Andrew Fisher, High Commissioner for Australia in the United Kingdom;

for the Union of South Africa:
Mr. Reginald Andrew Blankenberg, O.B.E., Acting High Commissioner for the Union of South Africa in the United Kingdom;

for the Dominion of New Zealand:
The Honourable Sir Thomas Mackenzie, K.C.M.G., High Commissioner for New Zealand in the United Kingdom;

for India:
Sir Eyre Crowe, K.C.B., K.C.M.G.

The President of the French Republic:
Mr. Georges Clemenceau, President of the Council, Minister of War;
Mr. Stephen Pichon, Minister for Foreign Affairs;
Mr. Louis-Lucien Klotz, Minister of Finance;
Mr. André Tardieu, Commissary General for Franco-American Military Affairs;
Mr. Jules Cambon, Ambassador of France;

His Majesty the King of Italy:
The Honourable Maggiorino Ferraris, Senator of the Kingdom;
The Honourable Guglielmo Marconi, Senator of the Kingdom;
Sir Giacomo de Martino, Envoy Extraordinary and Minister Plenipotentiary;

His Majesty the Emperor of Japan:
Mr. K.Matsui, Ambassador Extraordinary and Plenipotentiary of H.M. the Emperor of Japan at Paris;

His Majesty the King of the Belgians:

Mr. Jules van den Heuvel, Envoy Extraordinary and Minister Plenipotentiary, Minister of State;

Mr. Rolin-Jaequemyns, Member of the Institute of Private International Law, Secretary-General of the Belgian Delegation;

The President of the Chinese Republic:
Mr. Vikyuin Wellington Koo;
Mr. Sao-ke Alfred Sze;

The President of the Cuban Republic:
Dr. Rafael Martinez Ortiz, Envoy Extraordinary and Minister Plenipotentiary of the Cuban Republic at Paris;

His Majesty the King of the Hellenes:
Mr. Elefthérios Venizelos, President of the Council of Ministers;
Mr. Nicolas Politis, Minister for Foreign Affairs;

His Majesty the King of the Hedjaz:
Mr. Rustem Haidar;
Mr. Abdul Hadi Aouni;

The President of the Polish Republic:
Mr. Ladislas Grabski;
Mr. Stanislas Patek, Minister Plenipotentiary;

The President of the Portuguese Republic:
Dr. Affonso Da Costa, formerly President of the Council of Ministers;
Mr. Jayme Batalha Reis, Minister Plenipotentiary;

His Majesty the King of Roumania:
Mr. Victor Antonesco, Envoy Extraordinary and Minister Plenipotentiary of H.M. the King of Roumania at Paris;

General Constantin Coanda, Corps Commander, A.D.C. to the King, formerly President of the Council of Ministers;

His Majesty the King of the Serbs, the Croats, and the Slovenes:

Mr. Nicolas P. Pachictch, formerly President of the Council of Ministers;

Mr. Ante Trumbic, Minister for Foreign Affairs;

Mr. Ivan Zolger, Doctor of Law;

His Majesty the King of Siam:

His Highness Prince Charoon, Envoy Extraordinary and Minister Plenipotentiary of H.M. the King of Siam at Paris;

The President of the Czecho-Slovak Republic:

Mr. Eduard Benes, Minister for Foreign Affairs;

Mr. Stephen Osusky, Envoy Extraordinary and Minister Plenipotentiary of the Czecho-Slovak Republic at London;

Bulgaria:

Mr. Alexander Stamboliski, President of the Council of Ministers, Minister of War;

Who, having communicated their full powers, found in good and due form, have agreed as follows:

From the coming into force of the present Treaty the state of war will terminate.

From that moment, and subject to the provisions of the present Treaty, official relations will exist between the Allied and Associated Powers and Bulgaria.

PART I.

THE COVENANT OF THE LEAGUE OF NATIONS
Articles 1 to 26 and Annex
[...]

PART II.

FRONTIERS OF BULGARIA.

ARTICLE 27.

The frontiers of Bulgaria shall be fixed as follows:

1.*With the Serb-Croat-Slovene State:* [...]

2.*With Greece:*

From the point defined above eastwards to the point where it leaves the watershed between the basins of the Mesta-Karasu on the south and the Maritsa (Marica) on the north near point 1587 (Dibikli),
    the frontier of 1913 between Bulgaria and Greece,

3. On the South, with territories which shall be subsequently attributed by the Principal Allied and Associated Powers:

Thence eastwards to point 1295 situated about 18 kilometres west of Kuchuk-Derbend,
    a line to be fixed on the ground following the watershed between the basin of the Maritsa on the north, and the basins of the Mesta-Karasu and the other rivers which flow directly into the Aegean Sea on the south;

thence eastwards to a point to be chosen on the frontier of 1913 between Bulgaria and Turkey about 4 kilometres north of Kuchuk-Derbend,

a line to be fixed on the ground following as nearly as possible the crest line forming the southern limit of the basin of the Akcehisar (Dzuma) Suju;

thence northwards to the point where it meets the river Maritsa,

the frontier of 1913;

thence to a point to be chosen about 3 kilometres below the railway station of Hadi-K. (Kadikoj),

the principal course of the Maritsa downstream;

thence northwards to a point to be chosen on the apex of the salient formed by the frontier of the Treaty of Sofia, 1915, about 10 kilometres east-south-east of Jisr Mustafa Pasha,

a line to be fixed on the ground;

thence eastwards to the Black Sea,

the frontier of the Treaty of Sofia, 1915, then the frontier of 1913.

4. The Black Sea: [...]

5.With Roumania: [...]

PART III.

POLITICAL CLAUSES

SECTION I.

SERB-CROAT- SLOVENE STATE.
[...]

SECTION II.

GREECE.

ARTICLE 42.

Bulgaria renounces in favour of Greece all rights and title over the territories of the Bulgarian Monarchy situated outside the frontiers of Bulgaria as laid down in Article 27, Part II (Frontiers of Bulgaria), and recognised by the present Treaty, or by any Treaties concluded for the purpose of completing the present settlement, as forming part of Greece.

ARTICLE 43.

A Commission consisting of seven members, five nominated by the Principal Allied and Associated Powers, one by Greece, and one by Bulgaria, will be appointed fifteen days after the coming into force of the present Treaty to trace on the spot the frontier line described in Article 27 (2), Part II (Frontiers of Bulgaria), of the present Treaty.

ARTICLE 44.

Bulgarian nationals habitually resident in the territories assigned to Greece will obtain Greek nationality *ipso facto* and will lose their Bulgarian nationality.

Bulgarian nationals, however, who became resident in these territories after January 1, 1913, will not acquire Greek nationality without a permit from Greece.

ARTICLE 45.

Within a period of two years from the coming into force of the present Treaty, Bulgarian nationals over 18 years of age and habitually resident in the territories assigned to Greece in accordance with the present Treaty will be entitled to opt for Bulgarian nationality.

Option by husband will cover his wife and option by parents will cover their children under 18 years of age.

Persons who have exercised the above right to opt must within the succeeding twelve months transfer their place of residence to the State for which they have opted.

They will be entitled to retain their immovable property in the territory of the other State where they had their place of residence before exercising their right to opt. They may carry with them their movable property of every description. No export or import duties may be imposed upon them in connection with the removal of such property.

ARTICLE 46.

Greece accepts and agrees to embody in a Treaty with the Principal Allied and Associated Powers such provisions as may be deemed necessary by these Powers to protect the interests of inhabitants of that State who differ from the majority of the population in race, language or religion.

Greece further accepts and agrees to embody in a Treaty with the Principal Allied and Associated Powers such provisions as these Powers may deem necessary to protect freedom of transit and equitable treatment for the commerce of other nations.

ARTICLE 47.

The proportion and nature of the financial obligations of Bulgaria which Greece will have to assume on account of the territory placed under her sovereignty will de determined in accordance with Article 141, Part VIII (Financial Clauses), of the present Treaty.

Subsequent agreements will decide all questions which are not decided by the present Treaty and which may arise in consequence of the cession of the said territory.

SECTION III.

THRACE.

ARTICLE 48.

Bulgaria renounces in favour of the Principal Allied and Associated Powers all rights and title over the territories in Thrace which belonged to the Bulgarian Monarchy and which, being situated outside the new frontiers of Bulgaria as described in Article 27 (3), Part II (Frontiers of Bulgaria), have not been at present assigned to any State.

Bulgaria undertakes to accept the settlement made by the Principal Allied and Associated Powers in regard to these territories, particularly in so far as concerns the nationality of the inhabitants.

The Principal Allied and Associated Powers undertake to ensure the economic outlets of Bulgaria to the Aegean Sea.

The conditions of this guarantee will be fixed at a later date.

SECTION IV.

PROTECTION OF MINORITIES.
[...]

SECTION V.

GENERAL PROVISIONS.
[...]

ARTICLE 59.

Bulgaria hereby recognises and accepts the frontiers of Austria, Greece, Hungary, Poland, Roumania, the Serb-Croat-Slovene State and the Czecho-Slovak State as these frontiers may be determined by the Principal Allied and Associated Powers.

PART IV.

MILITARY, NAVAL AND AIR CLAUSES.
[...]

PART V.

PRISONERS OF WAR AND GRAVES.
[...]

PART VI.

PENALTIES.
[...]

PART VII.

REPARATION.
[...]

ARTICLE 126.

Bulgaria undertakes to seek for and forthwith to return to Greece, Roumania, and the Serb-Croat-Slovene State respectively any records or archives or any articles of archaeological, historic or artistic interest which have been taken away from the territories of those countries during the present war.

Any dispute between the Powers above named and Bulgaria as to their ownership of any such articles shall be referred to an arbitrator to be appointed by the Inter-Allied Commission, and whose decision shall be final.
[...]

PART VIII.

FINANCIAL CLAUSES.
[...]

PART IX.

ECONOMIC CLAUSES.
[...]

PART X.

AERIAL NAVIGATION.
[...]

PART XI.

PORTS, WATERWAYS AND RAILWAYS.
[...]

PART XII.

LABOUR.
[...]

PART XIII.

MISCELLANEOUS PROVISIONS.
[...]

ARTICLE 296.
[...]

The present Treaty, in French, in English, and in Italian, shall be ratified. In case of divergence, the French text shall prevail except in Parts I (Covenant of the League of Nations) and XII (Labour), where the French and English texts shall be of equal force.

The deposit of ratifications shall be made at Paris as soon as possible.

Powers of which the seat of the Government is outside Europe will be entitled merely to inform the Government of the French Republic through their diplomatic representative at Paris that their ratification has been given; in that case they must transmit the instrument of ratification as soon as possible.

A first procès-verbal of the deposit of ratifications will be drawn up as soon as the Treaty has been ratified by Bulgaria on the one hand, and by three of the Principal Allied and Associated Powers on the other hand.

From the date of this first procès-verbal the Treaty will come into force between the High Contracting Parties who have ratified it. For the determination of all periods of time provided for in the present Treaty this date will be the date of the coming into force of the Treaty.

In all other respects the Treaty will enter into force for each Power at the date of the deposit of its ratification.

The French Government will transmit to all the signatory Powers a certified copy of the procès-verbaux of the deposit of ratifications.

In Faith whereof the above-named Plenipotentiaries have signed the present Treaty.

Done at Neuilly-sur-Seine, the twenty-seventh day of November, one thousand nine hundred and nineteen, in a single copy which will remain deposited in the archives of the French Republic, and of which authenticated copies will be transmitted to each of the Signatory Powers.

(L.S.) Frank L. Polk.
(L.S.) Henry White.
(L.S.) Tasker H. Bliss.
(L.S.) Cecil Harmsworh.
(L.S.) Eyre A. Crowe.
(L.S.) George H. Perley.
(L.S.) Andrew Fisher.
(L.S.) Thomas Mackenzie.
(L.S.) R. A. Blankenberg.
(L.S.) Eyre A. Crowe.
(L.S.) G. Clemenceau.
(L.S.) S. Pichon.
(L.S.) L. -L. Klotz.
(L.S.) Andre Tardieu.
(L.S.) Jules Cambon.
(L.S.) Guglielmo Marconi.

(L.S.) G. de Martino.
(L.S.) K. Matsui.
(L.S.) J. Van Den Heuvel.
(L.S.) Rolin-Jaequemyns.
(L.S.) Virkyuin Wellington Koo.
(L.S.) Rafael Martinez Ortiz.
(L.S.) Eleftherios Venizelos.
(L.S.) N. Politis.
(L.S.) M. Rustem Haidar.
(L.S) Aouni Abdul-Hadi.
(L.S.) L. Grabski.
(L.S.) St. Patek.
(L.S.) Affonso Costa.
(L.S) Jayme Batalha Reis.
(L.S.) Nik. P. Patchitch.
(L.S.) Dr. Ante Trumbic.
(L.S.) Dr. Ivan Zolger.
(L.S.) Charoon.
(L.S.) Dr. Edvard Benes.
(L.S.) Stefan Osusky.
(L.S.) Al. Stamboliiski.

TREATY OF LAUSANNE

(24 July 1923)

THE LAUSANNE CONFERENCE, *which convened in order to revise the Treaty of Sèvres (10 August 1920), had been provided for in the Armistice of Mudania (11 October 1922). It lasted from 20 November 1922 to 24 July 1923, with a short break of two and a half months from February to April.*

Representatives of eight countries took part in the proceedings: Great Britain, France, Italy, Japan, Roumania, Serbia, Greece and Turkey. The United States also participated, as an observer.

The British, French and Italian delegations were headed by their Foreign Ministers,[1] while the delegations of Turkey and Greece were headed by Ismet Pasha[2] and El. Venizelos respectively.[3]

The Prime Ministers of France and Italy, Poincaré and Mussolini, attended the opening session of the conference, at the Casino Mont Benon in Lausanne. English, French and Italian were designated as the official languages for the remainder of the conference, held in the Hôtel du Chateau, Lausanne.

---

1. Curzon, Barrera and Garroni, respectively. During the second phase of the conference, they were replaced by Sir George Rumbold, Montagna and Pellé, while Child, the American observer, was replaced by Ambassador Clark, the U.S. diplomatic representative in Switzerland.

2. Later Inönü.

3. Venizelos was recalled to assume the co-ordination of the Greek delegation for the negotiations at this very difficult juncture for the nation. The Greek delegation also included Ambassadors Dimitrios Kaklamanos (London) and Athos Romanos (Paris), together with Andreas Michalakopoulos, Alexander Mazarakis-Ainian (military adviser), Michael G. Theotokas (legal adviser), Emmanouil Repoulis and Nicolaos Politis. Foreign Minister Apostolos Alexandris took part in the second phase of the conference.

In its final form, the Treaty of Lausanne consisted of 143 articles. Three conventions[4] and two protocols were signed along with it. Although, in its final article, the Treaty laid down that its ratification was to begin as soon as possible, in practice this did not prove feasible until August 1924.

The Treaty of Lausanne ceded to Turkey all the territory held by Greece in Asia Minor, Eastern Thrace[5] (with Karagatch and the Arda-Evros triangle,[6] Imbros, Tenedos and the Rabbit Islands, while sovereignty over the remaining islands of the Eastern Mediterranean passed to Greece,[7] as specified in article 12. Finally, all Turkish titles and rights to the Dodecanese were transferred to Italy, along with the island of Castellorizo.[8] In effect, Greece failed to fulfil the national claims which

---

4. The Convention concerning the exchange of Greek and Turkish populations and the relative protocol (30 January 1923), the Convention concerning the regime of the Straits (24 July 1923), and the Convention on the border in Thrace (24 July 1923). A protocol on Karagatch and the islands of Imbros and Tenedos was signed by Great Britain, France, Italy, Japan, Greece and Turkey on 24 July 1923. The Convention of Lausanne imposed the demilitarisation of the Straits under the control of an international commission. This act which Turkey interpreted as an intrusion on her sovereign rights, was revised by the Convention of Montreux (20/7/1936). This was a significant diplomatic success for Turkey. However, the revision of the Lausanne Convention proved to be a setback for the allies, since Turkey, throughout the duration of the war, refused passage through the Straits to allied vessels. The Germans, on the other hand, were permitted to use the Straits for the passage and refuelling of their merchant vessels and warships.

5. Already ceded to Turkey by the Mudania Armistice.

6. Although during the course of the conference Turkey suddenly proposed a return to the borders agreed by the Treaty of Bucharest, the Greek-Turkish frontier was eventually fixed at the middle of the river Evros. The above frontier was defined in a special protocol signed by the two countries on 3 November 1926. See V. Vlangopoulos, *Key Treaties 1821-1967*, Thessaloniki, 1998, p. 310, (in Greek).

7. Greece had occupied the islands of the Aegean before the First Balkan War (October 1912), and de facto Greek sovereignty was recognised by the London Conference of ambassadors on 13 February 1914.

8. Italy's stance towards Greece throughout the conference was particularly hostile. It denounced all the treaties concerning the Dodecanese which Italy and Greece had signed up until that time.

had been satisfied by the Treaty of Sèvres (10 August 1920).[9] Venizelos, in a lengthy memorandum to the Allies (30 December 1918), had described in detail the distribution of the intrinsically Greek population which resided in areas adjacent to the Greek state.[10] However, the Sèvres Peace Treaty was never ratified by the contracting parties, and thus it was never enforced. For Turkey, the Treaty of Sèvres signalled the end of the Ottoman Empire; for Greece, impoverished and without any help from its allies, it left the country exposed to the perils of Kemalist nationalism. As a result, three years later, it lost at Lausanne precisely what it had gained at Sèvres.

---

9. The Treaty of Sèvres contained 433 articles and a large number of lengthy appendices. Along with it, three supplementary treaties were also signed (on Western Thrace, on the Dodecanese, and on the protection of ethnic minorities in Greece) and two conventions (on special rights of vigilance and control and on zones of influence in Turkey). Under the convention establishing the border in Thrace, the Powers made over to Greece the rights in Thrace which Bulgaria had ceded to them under the Treaty of Neuilly (Article 48). Although this convention was never ratified, it was kept in force by Special Protocol No. XVI of the Treaty of Lausanne (24 July 1923).

10. The memorandum presented the number of Greeks living in Asia Minor as 1,694,000.

TREATY* OF LAUSANNE

The British Empire, France, Italy, Japan, Greece, Roumania and the Serb-Croat-Slovene State of the one part, and Turkey of the other part;

Being united in the desire to bring to a final close the state of war which has existed in the East since 1914,

Being anxious to re-establish the relations of friendship and commerce which are essential to the mutual well-being of their respective peoples,

And considering that these relations must be based on respect for the independence and sovereignty of States,

Have decided to conclude a Treaty for this purpose, and have appointed as their Plenipotentiaries:

His Majesty the King of the United Kingdom of Great Britain and Ireland and of the British dominions beyond the Seas, Emperor of India:

The Right Honourable Sir Horace George Montagu Rumbold, Baronet, G.C.M.G., High Commissioner at Constantinople;

The President of the French Republic:

General Maurice Pellé, Ambassador of France, High Commissioner of the Republic in the East, Grand Officer of the National Order of the Legion of Honour;

---

* *The Treaties of Peace : 1919-1923,* Vol. II, New York : Carnegie Endowment Ed., 1924, pp. 959-1022.

His Majesty the King of Italy:

The Honourable Marquis Camillo Garroni, Senator of the Kingdom, Ambassador of Italy, High Commissioner at Constantinople, Grand Cross of the Orders of Saints Maurice and Lazarus, and of the Crown of Italy;

M. Giulio Cesare Montagna, Envoy Extraordinary and Minister Plenipotentiary at Athens, Commander of the Orders of Saints Maurice and Lazarus, Grand Officer of the Crown of Italy;

His Majesty the Emperor of Japan:

Mr. Kentaro Otchiai, Jusammi, First Class of the Order of the Rising Sun, Ambassador Extraordinary and Plenipotentiary at Rome;

His Majesty the King of the Hellenes:

M. Eleftherios K.Venisélos, formerly President of the Council of Ministers, Grand Cross of the Order of the Saviour;

M. Demetrios Caclamanos, Minister Plenipotentiary at London, Commander of the Order of the Saviour;

His Majesty the King of Roumania:

M. Constantine I. Diamandy, Minister Plenipotentiary;

M. Constantine Contzesco, Minister Plenipotentiary;

His Majesty the King of the Serbs, the Croats and the Slovenes:

Dr. Miloutine Yovanovitch, Envoy Extraordinary and Minister Plenipotentiary at Berne;

The Government of the Grand National Assembly of Turkey:

Ismet Pasha, Minister for Foreign Affairs, Deputy for Adrianople;

Dr. Riza Nour Bey, Minister for Health and for Public Assistance, Deputy for Sinope;

Hassan Bey, formerly Minister, Deputy for Trebizond;
Who, having produced their full powers, found in good and
due form, have agreed as follows:

PART I.

POLITICAL CLAUSES.

ARTICLE 1.

From the coming into force of the present Treaty, the state
of peace will be definitely re-established between the British
Empire, France, Italy, Japan, Greece, Roumania and the Serb-
Croat-Slovene State of the one part, and Turkey of the other part,
as well as between their respective nationals.

Official relations will be resumed on both sides and, in the
respective territories, diplomatic and consular representatives will
receive, without prejudice to such agreements as may be concluded
in the future, treatment in accordance with the general principles
of international law.

SECTION I.

1. TERRITORIAL CLAUSES.

ARTICLE 2.

From the Black Sea to the Aegean the frontier of Turkey is
laid down as follows:

(1) With Bulgaria:
From the mouth of the River Rezvaya, to the River Maritza,

the point of junction of the three frontiers of Turkey, Bulgaria and Greece:
    the southern frontier of Bulgaria as at present demarcated ;

(2)With Greece:
Thence to the confluence of the Arda and the Maritza:
    the course of the Maritza;
    then upstream along the Arda, up to a point on that river to be determined on the spot in the immediate neighbourhood of the village of Tchörek-Keuy;
    the course of the Arda;
    thence in a south-easterly direction up to a point on the Maritza, 1 kilom. below Bosna-Keuy:
    a roughly straight line leaving in Turkish terrritory the village of Bosna-Keuy. The village of Tchörek-Keuy shall be assigned to Greece or to Turkey according as the majority of the population shall be found to be Greek or Turkish by the Commission for which provision is made in Article 5, the population which has migrated into this village after the 11th October, 1922, not being taken into account;
    thence to the Aegean Sea:
    the course of the Maritza.

ARTICLE 3.

From the Mediterranean to the frontier of Persia, the frontier of Turkey is laid down as follows:

(1) With Syria:
The frontier described in Article 8 of the Franco-Turkish Agreement of the 20th October, 1921;

(2)With Iraq:

The frontier between Turkey and Iraq shall be laid down in friendly arrangement to be concluded between Turkey and Great Britain within nine months.

In the event of no agreement being reached between the two Governments within the time mentioned, the dispute shall be referred to the Council of the League of Nations.

The Turkish and British Governments reciprocally undertake that, pending the decision to be reached on the subject of the frontier, no military or other movement shall take place which might modify in any way the present state of the territories of which the final fate will depend upon that decision.

ARTICLE 4.

The frontiers described by the present Treaty are traced on the one-in-a-million maps attached to the present Treaty. In case of divergence between the text and the map, the text will prevail. [See Introduction.]

ARTICLE 5.

A Boundary Commission will be appointed to trace on the ground the frontier defined in Article 2 (2). This Commission will be composed of representatives of Greece and of Turkey, each Power appointing one representative, and a president chosen by them from the nationals of a third Power.

They shall endeavour in all cases to follow as nearly as possible the descriptions given in the present Treaty, taking into account as far as possible administrative boundaries and local economic interests.

The decision of the Commission will be taken by a majority and shall be binding on the parties concerned.

The expenses of the Commission shall be borne in equal shares by the parties concerned.

ARTICLE 6.

In so far as concerns frontiers defined by a waterway as distinct from its banks, the phrases «course» or «channel» used in the descriptions of the present Treaty signify, as regards non-navigable rivers, the median line of the waterway or of its principal branch, and, as regards navigable rivers, the median line of the principal channel of navigation. It will rest with the Boundary Commission to specify whether the frontier line shall follow any changes of the course or channel which may take place, or whether it shall be definitely fixed by the position of the course or channel at the time when the present Treaty comes into force.

In the absence of provisions to the contrary, in the present Treaty, islands and islets lying within three miles of the coast are included within the frontier of the coastal State.

ARTICLE 7.

The various States concerned undertake to furnish to the Boundary Commission all documents necessary for its task, especially authentic copies of agreements fixing existing or old frontiers, all large scale maps in existence, geodetic data, surveys completed but unpublished, and information concerning the changes of frontier watercourses. The maps, geodetic data, and surveys, even if unpublished, which are in the possession of the Turkish authorities, must be delivered at Constantinople with the least possible delay from the coming into force of the present Treaty to the President of the Commission.

The States concerned also undertake to instruct the local

authorities to communicate to the Commission all documents, especially plans, cadastral and land books, and to furnish on demand all details regarding property, existing economic conditions and other necessary information.

ARTICLE 8.

The various States interested undertake to give every assistance to the Boundary Commission, whether directly or through local authorities, in everything that concerns transport, accomodation, labour, materials (sign posts, boundary pillars) necessary for the accomplishment of its mission.

In particular, the Turkish Government undertakes to furnish, if required, the technical personnel necessary to assist the Boundary Commission in the accomplishment of its duties.

ARTICLE 9.

The various States interested undertake to safeguard the trigonometrical points, signals, posts or frontier marks erected by the Commission.

ARTICLE 10.

The pillars will be placed so as to be intervisible. They will be numbered, and their position and their number will be noted on a cartographic document.

ARTICLE 11.

The protocols defining the boundary and the maps and

documents attached thereto will be made out in triplicate, of which two copies will be forwarded to the Governments of the limitrophe States, and the third to the Government of the French Republic, which will deliver authentic copies to the Powers who sign the present Treaty.

ARTICLE 12.

The decision taken on the 13th February 1914, by the Conference of London, in virtue of Articles 5 of the Treaty of London of the 17th-30th May, 1913, and 15 of the Treaty of Athens of the 1st-14th November, 1913, which decision was communicated to the Greek Government on the 13th February 1914, regarding the sovereignty of Greece over the islands of the Eastern Mediterranean, other than the islands of Imbros, Tenedos and Rabbit Islands, particularly the islands of Lemnos, Samothrace, Mytilene, Chios, Samos and Nikaria, is confirmed, subject to the provisions of the present Treaty respecting the islands placed under the sovereignty of Italy which form the subject of Article 15.

Except where a provision to the contrary is contained in the present Treaty, the islands situated at less than three miles from the Asiatic coast remain under Turkish sovereignty.

ARTICLE 13.

With a view to ensuring the maintenance of peace, the Greek Government undertakes to observe the following restrictions in the islands of Mytilene, Chios, Samos and Nikaria:

(1) No naval base and no fortification will be established in the said islands.

(2) Greek military aircraft will be forbidden to fly over the

territory of the Anatolian coast. Reciprocally, the Turkish Government will forbid their military aircraft to fly over the said islands.

(3) The Greek military forces in the said islands will be limited to the normal contingent called up for military service, which can be trained on the spot, as well as to a force of gendarmerie and police in proportion to the force of gendarmerie and police existing in the whole of the Greek territory.

ARTICLE 14.

The islands of Imbros and Tenedos, remaining under Turkish sovereignty, shall enjoy a special administrative organisation composed of local elements and furnishing every guarantee for the native non-Moslem population in so far as concerns local administration and the protection of persons and property. The maintenance of order will be assured therein by a police force recruited from amongst the local population by the local administration above provided for and placed under its orders.

The agreements which have been, or may be, concluded between Greece and Turkey relating to the exchange of the Greek and Turkish populations will not be applied to the inhabitants of the islands of Imbros and Tenedos.

ARTICLE 15.

Turkey renounces in favour of Italy all rights and title over the following islands: Stampalia (Astrapalia), Rhodes (Rhodos), Calki (Kharki), Scarpanto, Casos (Casso), Piscopis (Tilos), Misiros (Nisyros), Calimnos (Kalymnos), Leros, Patmos, Lipsos (Lipso), Simi (Symi), and Cos (Kos), which are now occupied by Italy, and the islets dependent thereon, and also over the island of Castellorizzo.

ARTICLE 16.

Turkey hereby renounces all rights and title whatsoever over or respecting the territories situated outside the frontiers laid down in the present Treaty and the islands other than those over which her sovereignty is recognised by the said Treaty, the future of these territories and islands being settled or to be settled by the parties concerned.

The provisions of the present Article do not prejudice any special arrangements arising from neighbourly relations which have been or may be concluded between Turkey and any limitrophe countries.

ARTICLE 17.

The renunciation by Turkey of all rights and titles over Egypt and over the Soudan will take effect as from the 5th November, 1914.

ARTICLE 18.

Turkey is released from all undertakings and obligations in regard to the Ottoman Ioans guaranteed on the Egyptian tribute, that is to say, the loans of 1855, 1891 and 1894. The annual payments made by Egypt for the service of these loans now forming part of the service of the Egyptian Public Debt, Egypt is freed from all other obligations relating to the Ottoman Public Debt.

ARTICLE 19.

Any questions arising from the recognition of the State of Egypt shall be settled by agreements to be negotiated subsequently in a manner to be determined later between the Powers concerned. The provisions of the present Treaty relating to territories detached from Turkey under the said Treaty will not apply to Egypt.

ARTICLE 20.

Turkey hereby recognises the annexation of Cyprus proclaimed by the British Government on the 5th November, 1914.

ARTICLE 21.

Turkish nationals ordinarily resident in Cyprus on the 5th November, 1914, will acquire British nationality subject to the conditions laid down in the local law, and will thereupon lose their Turkish nationality. They will, however, have the right to opt for Turkish nationality within two years from the coming into force of the present Treaty, provided that they leave Cyprus within twelve months after having so opted.

Turkish nationals ordinarily resident in Cyprus on the coming into force of the present Treaty who, at that date, have acquired or are in process of acquiring British nationality, in consequence of a request made in accordance with the local law, will also thereupon lose their Turkish nationality.

It is understood that the Government of Cyprus will be entitled to refuse British nationality to inhabitants of the island who, being Turkish nationals, had formerly acquired another nationality without the consent of the Turkish Government.

ARTICLE 22.

Without prejudice to the general stipulations of Article 27,

Turkey hereby recognises the definite abolition of all rights and privileges whatsoever which she enjoyed in Libya under the Treaty of Lausanne of the 18th October, 1912, and the instruments connected therewith.

2. SPECIAL PROVISIONS.

ARTICLE 23.

The High Contracting Parties are agreed to recognise and declare the principle of freedom of transit and of navigation, by sea and by air, in time of peace as in time of war, in the strait of the Dardanelles, the Sea of Marmora and the Bosphorus, as prescribed in the separate Convention signed this day, regarding the régime of the Straits. This Convention will have the same force and effect in so far as the present High Contracting Parties are concerned as if it formed part of the present Treaty.

ARTICLE 24.

The separate Convention signed this day respecting the régime for the frontier described in Article 2 of the present Treaty will have equal force and effect in so far as the present High Contracting Parties are concerned as if it formed part of the present Treaty.

ARTICLE 25.

Turkey undertakes to recognise the full force of the Treaties of Peace and additional Conventions concluded by the other Contracting Powers with the Powers who fought on the side of

Turkey, and to recognise whatever dispositions have been or may be made concerning the territories of the former German Empire, of Austria, of Hungary and of Bulgaria, and to recognise the new States within their frontiers as there laid down.

ARTICLE 26.

Turkey hereby recognises and accepts the frontiers of Germany, Austria, Bulgaria, Greece, Hungary, Poland, Roumania, the Serb-Croat-Slovene State and the Czechoslovak State, as these frontiers have been or may be determined by the Treaties referred to in Article 25 or by any supplementary conventions.

ARTICLE 27.

No power or jurisdiction in political, legislative or administrative matters shall be exercised outside Turkish territory by the Turkish Government or authorities, for any reason whatsoever, over the nationals of a territory placed under the sovereignty or protectorate of the other Powers signatory of the present Treaty, or over the nationals of a territory detached from Turkey.

It is understood that the spiritual attributions of the Moslem religious authorities are in no way infringed.

ARTICLE 28.

Each of the High Contracting Parties hereby accepts, in so far as it is concerned, the complete abolition of the Capitulations in Turkey in every respect.

ARTICLE 29.

Moroccans, who are French nationals («ressortissants») and Tunisians shall enjoy in Turkey the same treatment in all respects as other French nationals («ressortissants»).

Natives («ressortissants») of Libya shall enjoy in Turkey the same treatment in all respects as other Italian nationals («ressortissants»).

The stipulations of the present Article in no way prejudge the nationality of persons of Tunisian, Libyan and Moroccan origin established in Turkey.

Reciprocally, in the territories the inhabitants of which benefit by the stipulations of the first and second paragraphs of this Article, Turkish nationals shall benefit by the same treatment as in France and in Italy respectively.

The treatment to which merchandise originating in or destined for the territories, the inhabitants of which benefit from the stipulations of the first paragraph of this Article, shall be subject in Turkey, and, reciprocally, the treatment to which merchandise originating in or destined for Turkey shall be subject in the said territories shall be settled by agreement between the French and Turkish Governments.

SECTION II.
_____

NATIONALITY.
_____

ARTICLE 30.

Turkish subjects habitually resident in territory which in accordance with the provisions of the present Treaty is detached from Turkey will become *ipso facto*, in the conditions laid down by the local law, nationals of the State to which such territory is transferred.

ARTICLE 31.

Persons over eighteen years of age, losing their Turkish nationality and obtaining *ipso facto* a new nationality under Article 30, shall be entitled within a period of two years from the coming into force of the present Treaty to opt for Turkish nationality.

ARTICLE 32.

Persons over eighteen years of age, habitually resident in territory detached from Turkey in accordance with the present Treaty, and differing in race from the majority of the population of such territory shall, within two years from the coming into force of the present Treaty, be entitled to opt for the nationality of one of the States in which the majority of the population is of the same race as the person exercising the right to opt, subject to the consent of that State.

ARTICLE 33.

Persons who have exercised the right to opt in accordance with the provisions of Articles 31 and 32 must, within the succeeding twelve months, transfer their place of residence to the State for which they have opted.

They will be entitled to retain their immovable property in the territory of the other State where they had their place of residence before exercising their right to opt.

They may carry with them their movable property of every description. No export or import duties may be imposed upon them in connection with the removal of such property.

A R T I C L E   3 4 .

Subject to any agreements which it may be necessary to conclude between the Governments exercising authority in the countries detached from Turkey and the Governments of the countries where the persons concerned are resident, Turkish nationals of over eighteen years of age who are natives of a territory detached from Turkey under the present Treaty, and who on its coming into force are habitually resident abroad, may opt for the nationality of the territory of which they are natives, if they belong by race to the majority of the population of that territory, and subject to the consent of the Government exercising authority therein. This right of option must be exercised within two years from the coming into force of the present Treaty.

A R T I C L E   3 5 .

The Contracting Powers undertake to put no hindrance in the way of the exercise of the right which the persons concerned have under the present Treaty, or under the Treaties of Peace concluded with Germany, Austria, Bulgaria or Hungary, or under any Treaty concluded by the said Powers, other than Turkey, or any of them, with Russia, or between themselves, to choose any other nationality which may be open to them.

A R T I C L E   3 6 .

For the purposes of the provisions of this Section, the status of a married woman will be governed by that of her husband, and the status of children under eighteen years of age by that of their parents.

SECTION III.

PROTECTION OF MINORITIES.

ARTICLE 37.

Turkey undertakes that the stipulations contained in Articles 38 to 44 shall be recognised as fundamental laws, and that no law, no regulation, nor official action shall conflict or interfere with these stipulations, nor shall any law, regulation, nor official action prevail over them.

ARTICLE 38.

The Turkish Government undertakes to assure full and complete protection of life and liberty to all inhabitants of Turkey without distinction of birth, nationality, language, race or religion.

All inhabitants of Turkey shall be entitled to free exercise, whether in public or private, of any creed, religion or belief, the observance of which shall not be incompatible with public order and good morals.

Non-Moslem minorities will enjoy full freedom of movement and of emigration, subject to the measures applied, on the whole or on part of the territory, to all Turkish nationals, and which may be taken by the Turkish Government for national defence, or for the maintenance of public order.

ARTICLE 39.

Turkish nationals belonging to non-Moslem minorities will enjoy the same civil and political rights as Moslems.

All the inhabitants of Turkey, without distinction of religion, shall be equal before the law.

Differences of religion, creed or confession shall not prejudice any Turkish national in matters relating to the enjoyment of civil or political rights, as, for instance, admission to public employments, functions and honours, or the exercise of professions and industries.

No restrictions shall be imposed on the free use by any Turkish national of any language in private intercourse, in commerce, religion, in the press, or in publications of any kind or at public meetings.

Notwithstanding the existence of the official language, adequate facilities shall be given to Turkish nationals of non-Turkish speech for the oral use of their own language before the Courts.

ARTICLE 40.

Turkish nationals belonging to non-Moslem minorities shall enjoy the same treatment and security in law and in fact as other Turkish nationals. In particular, they shall have an equal right to establish, manage and control at their own expense, any charitable, religious and social institutions, any schools and other establishments for instruction and education, with the right to use their own language and to exercise their own religion freely therein.

ARTICLE 41.

As regards public instruction, the Turkish Government will grant in those towns and districts, where a considerable proportion of non-Moslem nationals are resident, adequate facilities for ensuring that in the primary schools the instruction shall be given to the children of such Turkish nationals through the medium of their own language. This provision will not prevent the Turkish

Government from making the teaching of the Turkish language obligatory in the said schools.

In towns and districts where there is a considerable proportion of Turkish nationals belonging to non-Moslem minorities, these minorities shall be assured an equitable share in the enjoyment and application of the sums which may be provided out of public funds under the State, municipal or other budgets for educational, religious, or charitable purposes.

The sums in question shall be paid to the qualified representatives of the establishments and institutions concerned.

ARTICLE 42.

The Turkish Government undertakes to take, as regards non-Moslem minorities, in so far as concerns their family law or personal status, measures permitting the settlement of these questions in accordance with the customs of those minorities.

These measures will be elaborated by special Commissions composed of representatives of the Turkish Government and of representatives of each of the minorities concerned in equal number. In case of divergence, the Turkish Government and the Council of the League of Nations will appoint in agreement an umpire chosen from amongst European lawyers.

The Turkish Government undertakes to grant full protection to the churches, synagogues, cemeteries, and other religious establishments of the above-mentioned minorities. All facilities and authorisation will be granted to the pious foundations, and to the religious and charitable institutions of the said minorities at present existing in Turkey, and the Turkish Government will not refuse, for the formation of new religious and charitable institutions, any of the necessary facilities which are guaranteed to other private institutions of that nature.

ARTICLE 43.

Turkish nationals belonging to non-Moslem minorities shall not be compelled to perform any act with constitutes a violation of their faith or religious observances, and shall not be placed under any disability by reason of their refusal to attend Courts of Law or to perform any legal business on their weekly day of rest.

This provision, however, shall not exempt such Turkish nationals from such obligations as shall be imposed upon all other Turkish nationals for the preservation of public order.

ARTICLE 44.

Turkey agrees that, in so far as the preceding Articles of this Section affect non-Moslem nationals of Turkey, these provisions constitute obligations of international concern and shall be placed under the guarantee of the League of Nations. They shall not be modified without the assent of the majority of the Council of the League of Nations. The British Empire, France, Italy and Japan hereby agree not to withhold their assent to any modification in these Articles which is in due form assented to by a majority of the Council of the League of Nations.

Turkey agrees that any Member of the Council of the League of Nations shall have the right to bring to the attention of the Council any infraction or danger of infraction of any of these obligations, and that the Council may thereupon take such action and give such directions as it may deem proper and effective in the circumstances.

Turkey further agrees that any difference of opinion as to questions of law or of fact arising out of these Articles between the Turkish Government and any one of the other Signatory Powers or any other Power, a member of the Council of the League of Nations, shall be held to be a dispute of an international character under Article 14 of the Covenant of the League of Nations. The Turkish Government hereby consents that any such dispute shall, if the other party thereto demands, be referred to the Permanent Court of International Justice. The decision of the Permanent Court shall be final and shall have the same force and effect as an award under Article 13 of the Covenant.

ARTICLE 45.

The rights conferred by the provisions of the present Section on the non-Moslem minorities of Turkey will be similarly conferred by Greece on the Moslem minority in her territory.

PART II.
_____

FINANCIAL CLAUSES.
[...]

PART III.
_____

ECONOMIC CLAUSES.
[...]

PART IV.
_____

COMMUNICATIONS AND SANITARY QUESTIONS.
[...]

PART V.

MISCELLANEOUS PROVISIONS.
[...]

SECTION III.

GENERAL PROVISIONS.
[...]

ARTICLE 143.

The present Treaty shall be ratified as soon as possible.

The ratifications shall be deposited at Paris.

The Japanese Government will be entitled merely to inform the Government of the French Republic through their diplomatic representative at Paris when their ratification has been given; in that case, they must transmit the instrument of ratification as soon as possible.

Each of the Signatory Powers will ratify by one single instrument the present Treaty and the other instruments signed by it and mentioned in the Final Act of the Conference of Lausanne, in so far as these require ratification.

A first *procès-verbal* of the deposit of ratifications shall be drawn up as soon as Turkey, on the one hand, and the British Empire, France, Italy and Japan, or any three of them, on the other hand, have deposited the instruments of their ratifications.

From the date of this first *procès-verbal* the Treaty will come into force between the High Contracting Parties who have thus ratified it. Thereafter it will come into force for the other Powers at the date of the deposit of their ratifications.

As between Greece and Turkey, however, the provisions of Articles 1, 2 (2) and 5-11 inclusive will come into force as soon as the Greek and Turkish Governments have deposited the instruments of their ratifications, even if at that time the *procès-verbal* referred to above has not yet been drawn up.

The French Government will transmit to all the Signatory Powers a certified copy of the *procès-verbaux* of the deposit of ratifications.

In faith whereof the above-named Plenipotentiaries have signed the present Treaty.

Done at Lausanne, the 24th July, 1923, in a single copy, which will de deposited in the archives of the Government of the French Republic, which will transmit a certified copy to each of the Contracting Powers.

(L.S.)HORACE RUMBOLD.
(L.S.)PELLE.
(L.S.)GARRONI.
(L.S.)G. C. MONTAGNA.
(L.S.)K. OTCHIAI.
(L.S.)E. K. VENISELOS.
(L.S.)D. CACLAMANOS.
(L.S.)CONST. DIAMANDY.
(L.S.)CONST. CONTZESCO.
( )..............................
(L.S.)M. ISMET.
(L.S.)DR. RIZA NOUR.
(L.S.)HASSAN.

TREATY OF PEACE WITH ITALY

(10 February 1947)

Twenty-one *states which had been at war with one or more of the Axis countries and had signed, correspondingly, one or more armistice agreements participated in the Paris Conference (29 July - 5 October 1946). Representatives of Italy, Bulgaria, Roumania and Albania were invited to attend for shorter periods and to provide clarifications on specific points.*

Greece was represented by a large national delegation headed by Prime Minister Constantinos Tsaldaris and also including members of the Opposition, since Greece wanted to make it plain that its national demands were unanimously supported.[1]

Greek expectations were not met by the Paris Peace Conference. Greece succeeded though in obtaining the Dodecanese which were ceded to it by Italy.[2] The cession of the Dodecanese was approved un-

---

1. See also, Constantopoulou Ph. & Divani L., (eds.), *The Dodecanese. The Long Road to Union with Greece*, Athens: Kastaniotis, 1997.

2. Although at the time of the War of Independence the islanders of the Dodecanese had hoped for union with Greece, the London Protocol left the group of islands outside the Greek frontiers. They remained under Ottoman occupation until 1912, when they were captured by Italy during the Italian-Turkish war. Although under the Treaty of Ouchy (15 October 1912), Italian occupation was temporary, Italy attained full sovereignty as a result of the secret London Treaty of 26 April 1915, in exchange for Italy's entry into the First World War on the side of the Entente. The Venizelos-Tittoni agreement of 29 July 1919 and the Treaty of Sèvres (10 August 1920) both provided for the cession of the islands to Greece (with the exception of Rhodes), but were never implemented, partly as a result of the Asia Minor disaster. Turkey finally and irrevocably renounced its

animously on 25 September 1946 by the Political and Territorial Commission for the Peace Treaty with Italy. The formal incorporation of the Dodecanese into Greece took place on 7 March 1948, at a ceremony in Rhodes.[3]

With the signature of the Paris Peace Treaty and the cession of the Dodecanese, Greece was subrogated as the successor state[4] to Italy in the agreements which the latter had signed with Turkey in 1932 concerning the determination of the exact boundary line between the Dodecanese, then under Italian rule, and Turkish territory.

Even after the signature of the Treaty of Lausanne, by which Turkey had renounced its rights to the Dodecanese, it still had claims on the group of the islands due to their strategic position and their proximity to the coast of Asia Minor.[5] As a result, Italy and Turkey signed a convention in Ankara on 4 January 1932 regarding the islets lying between the coast of Asia Minor and the island of Castellorizo, as well as the disputed sovereignty of Kara Ada island. The convention delineated the territorial waters of these islets, whose sovereignty had been a cause of dispute between the two countries.

---

rights to the Dodecanese in favour of Italy under the Lausanne Peace Treaty of 24 July 1923 (Article 15).

3. After the capitulation of Italy in September 1943, control over the Dodecanese passed to Germany. When Germany in turn capitulated, the islands passed into British hands, and it was from Britain that Greece formally took them over on 31 March 1947.

4. This is a classic instance of state succession, in treaties under which territory passes from the sovereignty of one state to that of another, as it is reflected under the customary International Law. For a detailed analysis of the question of succession in this instance, c.f. C.P. Economidés, Les îlots d'Imia dans la mer Egée: Un différend crée par la force, RGDIP, No. 2, April-June 1997, pp. 344-346.

5. The diplomatic dispute was over the sovereignty of certain islets dependent on the island of Castellorizo and lying between it and the Turkish coast. In May 1929, Italy and Turkey signed a Compromissum, by which they agreed to refer their dispute to the Permanent Court of International Justice at The Hague. However, subsequent to the signature of the two agreements cited above, Italy and Turkey applied for the case to be struck off the cause list of the Court, which declared the case closed on 26 January 1933.

On the same date, Italy and Turkey exchanged letters in which, on the one hand, confirmed that there were no outstanding points of dispute between the two countries in connection with their respective territorial sovereignties, and, on the other, they undertook to define the remaining part of the Italian-Turkish sea frontier, over which there had been no disagreement between them. This delineation was formalised in a procès-verbal signed by the contracting parties in Ankara on 28 December 1932.[6] That agreement ultimately determined the side to which most of the islands, islets and rocks of the area belonged. Among them, within the delineated territorial waters, were the Imia rocks (point 30 of the agreement of 28 December 1932), which were specified as belonging to Italy and thus subsequently to Greece.[7]

---

6. On 3 January 1933, the Turkish Foreign Minister sent a letter to the Italian Ambassador in Ankara, stating that the process of delineating the sea frontier between Italy and Turkey had been completed and embodied in a 'procès - verbal' signed by the representatives of the two states, and that Ankara approved the arrangement. This delineation was confirmed by the Regional Air Traffic Agreement adopted in Constantinople in 1950, by which Turkey accepted that sea frontiers already existed in the area. From a series of maps attached to that Agreement, it is evident that the Imia rocks belong to Greece.

7. See footnote No. 4

TREATY* OF PEACE WITH ITALY

The Union of Soviet Socialist Republics, the United Kingdom of Great Britain and Northern Ireland, the United States of America, China, France, Australia, Belgium, the Byelorussian Soviet Socialist Republic, Brazil, Canada, Czechoslovakia, Ethiopia, Greece, India, the Netherlands, New Zealand, Poland, the Ukrainian Soviet Socialist Republic, the Union of South Africa, and the People's Federal Republic of Yugoslavia, hereinafter referred to as 'the Allied and Associated Powers', of the one part, and Italy, of the other part:

Whereas Italy under the Fascist régime became a party to the Tripartite Pact with Germany and Japan, undertook a war of aggression and thereby provoked a state of war with all the Allied and Associated Powers and with other United Nations, and bears her share of responsibility for the war; and

Whereas in consequence of the victories of the Allied forces, and with the assistance of the democratic elements of the Italian people, the Fascist régime in Italy was overthrown on July 25, 1943, and Italy, having surrendered unconditionally, signed terms of Armistice on September 3 and 29 of the same year; and

Whereas after the said Armistice Italian armed forces, both of the Government and of the Resistance Movement, took and active part in the war against Germany, and Italy declared war on Germany as from October 13, 1943, and thereby became a co-belligerent against Germany; and

---

* *Treaties of Peace with Italy, Roumania, Bulgaria, Hungary and Finland,* London : Printed by His Majesty's Stationery Office, 1947, pp. 7-36.

Whereas the Allied and Associated Powers and Italy are desirous of concluding a treaty of peace which, in conformity with the principles of justice, will settle questions still outstanding as a result of the events herein-before recited and will form the basis of friendly relations between them, thereby enabling the Allied and Associated Powers to support Italy's application to become a member of the United Nations and also to adhere to any convention concluded under the auspices of the United Nations;

Have therefore agreed to declare the cessation of the state of war and for this purpose to conclude the present Treaty of Peace, and have accordingly appointed the undersigned Plenipotentiaries who, after presentation of their full powers, found in good and due form, have agreed on the following provisions:

PART I. TERRITORIAL CLAUSES

SECTION I. FRONTIERS
[...]

SECTION II. FRANCE
[...]

SECTION III. AUSTRIA
[...]

SECTION IV. PEOPLE' S FEDERAL REPUBLIC OF YUGOSLAVIA
[...]

SECTION V. GREECE (Special Clause)

ARTICLE 14

1. Italy hereby cedes to Greece in full sovereignty the Do-

decanese Islands indicated hereafter, namely Stampalia (Astro-palia), Rhodes (Rhodos), Calki (Kharki), Scarpanto, Casos (Casso), Piscopis (Tilos), Misiros (Nisyros), Calimnos (Kalymnos), Leros, Patmos, Lipsos (Lipso), Simi (Symi), Cos (Kos) and Castellorizo, as well as the adjacent islets.

2. These islands shall be and shall remain demilitarised.

3. The procedure and the technical conditions governing the transfer of these islands to Greece will be determined by agreement between the Governments of the United Kingdom and Greece and arrangements shall be made for the withdrawal of foreign troops not later than 90 days from the coming into force of the present Treaty.

PART II. POLITICAL CLAUSES

SECTION I. GENERAL CLAUSES

ARTICLE 15

Italy shall take all measures necessary to secure to all persons under Italian jurisdiction, without distinction as to race, sex, language or religion, the enjoyment of human rights and of the fundamental freedoms, including freedom of expression, of press and publication, of religious worship, of political opinion and of public meeting.

ARTICLE 16

Italy shall not prosecute or molest Italian nationals, in-cluding members of the armed forces, solely on the ground that during the period from June 10, 1940, to the coming into force of the present Treaty, they expressed sympathy with or took action in support of the cause of the Allied and Associated Powers.

ARTICLE 17

Italy, which, in accordance with Article 30 of the Armistice Agreement, has taken measures to dissolve the Fascist organizations in Italy, shall not permit the resurgence on Italian territory of such organizations, whether political, military or semi-military, whose purpose it is to deprive the people of their democratic rights.

ARTICLE 18

Italy undertakes to recognize the full force of the Treaties of Peace with Roumania, Bulgaria, Hungary and Finland and other agreements or arrangements which have been or will be reached by the Allied and Associated Powers in respect of Austria, Germany and Japan for the restoration of peace.

SECTION II. NATIONALITY. CIVIL AND POLITICAL RIGHTS

ARTICLE 19

1. Italian citizens who were domiciled on June 10, 1940, in territory transferred by Italy to another State under the present Treaty, and their children born after that date, shall, except as provided in the following paragraph, become citizens with full civil and political rights of the State to which the territory is transferred, in accordance with legislation to that effect to be introduced by that

State within three months from the coming into force of the present Treaty. Upon becoming citizens of the State concerned they shall lose their Italian citizenship.

2. The Government of the State to which the territory is transferred shall, by appropriate legislation within three months from the coming into force of the present Treaty, provide that all persons referred to in paragraph 1 over the age of eighteen years (or married persons whether under or over that age) whose customary language is Italian, shall be entitled to opt for Italian citizenship within a period of one year from the coming into force of the present Treaty. Any person so opting shall retain Italian citizenship and shall not be considered to have acquired the citizenship of the State to which the territory is transferred. The option of the husband shall not constitute an option on the part of the wife. Option on the part of the father, or, if the father is not alive, on the part of the mother, shall, however, automatically include all unmarried children under the age of eighteen years.

3. The State to which the territory is transferred may require those who take advantage of the option to move to Italy within a year from the date when the option was exercised.

4. The State to which the territory is transferred shall, in accordance with its fundamental laws, secure to all persons within the territory, without distinction as to race, sex, language or religion, the enjoyment of human rights and of the fundamental freedoms, including freedom of expression, of press and publication, of religious worship, of political opinion and of public meeting.

ARTICLE 20

1. Within a period of one year from the coming into force

of the present Treaty, Italian citizens over 18 years of age (or married persons whether under or over that age), whose customary language is one of the Yugoslav languages (Serb, Croat or Slovene), and who are domiciled on Italian territory may, upon filing a request with a Yugoslav diplomatic or consular representative in Italy, acquire Yugoslav nationality if the Yugoslav authorities accept their request.

2. In such cases, the Yugoslav Government will communicate to the Italian Government through the diplomatic channel lists of the persons who have thus acquired Yugoslav nationality. The persons mentioned in such lists will lose their Italian nationality on the date of such official communication.

3. The Italian Government may require such persons to transfer their residence to Yugoslavia within a period of one year from the date of such official communication.

4. For the purposes of this Article, the rules relating to the effect of options on wives and on children, set forth in Article 19, paragraph 2, shall apply.

5. The provisions of Annex XIV, paragraph 10 of the present Treaty, applying to the transfer of properties belonging to persons who opt for Italian nationality, shall equally apply to the transfer of properties belonging to persons who opt for Yugoslav nationality under this Article.

[...]

PART III. WAR CRIMINALS

[...]

PART IV. NAVAL, MILITARY AND AIR CLAUSES

[...]

PART V. WITHDRAWAL OF ALLIED FORCES

[...]

PART VI. CLAIMS ARISING OUT OF THE WAR

[...]

PART VII. PROPERTY, RIGHTS AND INTERESTS

[...]

PART VIII. GENERAL ECONOMIC RELATIONS

[...]

PART IX. SETTLEMENT OF DISPUTES

[...]

PART X. MISCELLANEOUS ECONOMIC PROVISIONS

[...]

PART XI. FINAL CLAUSES

[...]

ARTICLE 90

The present Treaty, of which the French, English and Russian texts are authentic, shall be ratified by the Allied and Associated Powers. It shall also be ratified by Italy. It shall come into force immediately upon the deposit of ratifications by the Union of Soviet Socialist Republics, by the United Kingdom of Great Britain and Northern Ireland, by the United States of America, and by France. The instruments of ratification shall, in the shortest time possible, be deposited with the Government of the French Republic.

With respect to each Allied or Associated Power whose instrument of ratification is thereafter deposited, the Treaty shall come into force upon the date of deposit. The present Treaty shall be deposited in the archives of the Government of the French Republic, which shall furnish certified copies to each of the signatory States.

In faith whereof the undersigned Plenipotentiaries have signed the present Treaty and have affixed thereto their seals.

Done in the city of Paris in the French, English, Russian and Italian languages, this tenth day of February, One Thousand Nine Hundred And Forty-seven.

TIME CHART

25 March 1821	Outbreak of the War of Independence. Oecumenical Patriarch Grigorios V is hanged by the Ottomans in Constantinople (10 April 1821, Sunday of Easter).
28 June 1821	The Russians issue an ultimatum to the Sultan - delivered by Count Stroganov, Ambassador in Constantinople - demanding the protection of the Christian subjects of the Ottoman Empire throughout the Balkans. The ultimatum brings the Eastern Question to the forefront.
Autumn 1822	The Congress of Verona. Castlereagh dies and is succeeded by George Canning. The Greek revolutionaries are recognised as belligerents. Conclusion of the first Greek loan, for £800,000.
2 December 1823	Proclamation of the Monroe Doctrine ('America for the Americans', and thus respect for all independent states throughout the world).
February 1825	The Conference of St. Petersburg attempts to resolve the Eastern Question without the participation of Britain, which disagrees with the Tsar's proposal for the formation of three tributary principalities to the Sultan in Greek territory. The Conference of June 1824, had preceeded the St. Petesburg meeting.
1 December 1825	Tsar Alexander I dies and is succeeded by his younger brother Nicholas.

4 April 1826	Secret protocol of St. Petersburg between Russia and Britain. This was to have great significance for Greek affairs since it creates a real prospect for the liberation of the Greeks.
6 July 1827	The Anglo-Franco-Russian concert seems determined to support the Greek cause and replaces the secret protocol of St. Petersburg with the London Treaty on which the Independence of Greece is based.
August 1827	Sudden death of George Canning.
20 October 1827	The naval battle of Navarino results in the complete destruction of a Turkish-Egyptian fleet. Negotiations begin in Constantinople between the Sultan and the Ambassadors of Britain, France and Russia. Greeted with indifference, the ambassadors withdraw from Constantinople and make their way to Poros.
6 January 1828	Ioannis Capodistrias arrives in Greece.
12 December 1828	The Poros Ambassadorial Conference between Britain, France and Russia. Preparations are made for the establishment of a new state within 'natural' borders.
22 March 1829	Signature of the London Protocol, laying down the conditions for renewed negotiations with the Sultan, to be carried out by the British and French Ambassadors (Guilleminot and Gordon), who are expected to return to Constantinople. The three protecting powers recommend the creation of a Greek state to the Ottoman Empire.
14 September 1829	The Peace Treaty of Adrianople ends the Russo-Turkish war. The Sultan is compelled to accede to the international instruments signed in London on 6 July 1827 and 22 March 1829 and thus to consent to the foundation of an autonomous Greek state.
3 February 1830	Britain, France and Russia sign the London

	Protocol; proclamation of the Independence of Greece.
21 May 1830	Leopold of Saxe-Coburg refuses to accept the Greek throne offered to him by the Great Powers.
9 October 1831	The first President of Greece is assassinated.
7 May 1832	Otto (Othon), second son of Ludwig I of Bavaria, is proclaimed in London as hereditary King of the Hellenes. Greece is referred to as «an independent state and a monarchy».
21 July 1832	The Ottoman Empire and representatives of the three protecting powers (Britain, Russia, France), finally recognise the Volos-Arta line as the northern border of the independent Greek state following the signature of the Arrangement of Constantinople which makes Greece the first independent Christian state in the Balkans. The Principality of Samos is founded, under a Christian Prince-Governor appointed by the Sultan, with annual tribute of 4,000 Turkish pounds.
30 August 1832	The Constantinople Arrangement is ratified by the signature of the London Protocol by Britain, France and Russia.
18 September 1834	Athens becomes the capital of the Greek state.
1 June 1835	Othon reaches majority; end of the Bavarian Regency.
15 July 1841	The Straits Convention is signed in London by Turkey and the five Great Powers(Russia, Great Britain, Austria, France & Prussia). The Bosphorus and the Hellespont will henceforth be closed to all foreign warships as long as the Ottoman Empire does not engage in hostilities. The treaty represents a victory for Palmerston and British foreign policy over the Russians.

Mid-January 1850	The port of Piraeus is blockaded by a powerful squadron of the British fleet subsequent to the Don Pacifico affair.
1853-1856	The Crimean War ends with the Treaty of Paris in 1856. The Ottoman Empire joins the family of European nations, while Austria, Britain and France seem prepared to guarantee its integrity and independence.
March 1855	Tsar Nicholas I dies.
18 February 1856	The Sultan issues the *Hatt-i-hümayun*, a decree reforming and reorganising the non-Muslim ethnic communities (*millet*).
14 January 1858	Failed assassination attempt against Napoleon III of France, supporter of the 'doctrine of the nations', and the Empress Eugenie.
Spring 1860	Italian revolutionaries join Garibaldi's volunteers and succeed in the establishment of the Kingdom of Italy (1861). Events in Italy have an immediate impact on the Balkans.
10 October 1862	Othon's inertia towards the liberation of the unredeemed Greeks and the lack of a successor to the throne intensify the atmosphere of popular dissatisfaction. Othon is deposed. A provisional government assumes power (11 October).
6 June 1863	King Frederick VII of Denmark accepts the crown of Greece on behalf of Prince George, who is a minor.
13 July 1863	Treaty of London. The treaty incorporates the Ionian Islands within the frontiers of Greece, and ratifies the acceptance of Prince George to assume the Greek throne.
1 August 1863	In a protocol signed in London, Austria, France, Prussia and Russia consent to the cession of the Ionian Islands by Britain to Greece.

14 November 1863	The treaty ceding the Ionian Islands to Greece is signed in London without the participation of a Greek delegate.
29 March 1864	The final treaty of union of the Ionian Islands to mainland Greece is signed in London. Greece is represented by Charilaos Trikoupis, who after negotiations achieves improvements to the treaty of 14 November 1863.
2 June 1864	Greece officially becomes sovereign of the Ionian Islands.
1866	The Cretan Question enters a crucial phase.
26 August 1867	Signature at Volslau in Austria of a secret treaty of alliance between Greece and Serbia by which the two countries undertook to go to war against the Ottoman Empire in order to liberate all the Christians of the Balkans.
Spring 1868	Assassination of Prince Michael of Serbia. The Serbs regard the Voslau Treaty as Prince Michael's personal enterprise. After his death, and because the treaty did not adhere to any constitutional formalities, they consider it as null and void.
January 1869	After a general amnesty is extended to the rebels of Crete, the Porte establishes a new system of administration for the island. The Paris Conference of January 1869 achieves a provisional cease-fire in Crete.
1870-1871	Franco-German War. Bismarck is succeding the title of German Emperor.
March 1870	The Sultan issues an edict (*firman*) recognising the autonomy of the Bulgarian Church. The Oecumenical Patriarchate refuses to establish a line of communications with the Bulgarian Exarchate.
27 April 1875	King George I assigns Charilaos Trikoupis the mandate to form an administration.

2 July 1876	In view of the breach of the Volslau Treaty of 1867, Greece declines to take part in the hostilities of the war between Serbia and the Ottoman Empire.
31 August 1876	Sultan Murat V deposed as insane. He is succeeded by Abdulhamit.
23 December 1876	The Sultan issues a constitution applicable to the entire Empire based on the liberal European principles of freedom, justice and equality. The representatives of the Powers, however, are not convinced of the sincerity of the Sultan's intentions.
1877-1878	Russo-Turkish War.
June 1877-early 1878	All-party government with Constantine Kanaris Prime Minister and Charilaos Trikoupis as Foreign Minister. Greece remains neutral during the war.
20 January 1878	Russian troops capture Adrianople. The all-party Greek government resigns and is replaced by an administration with Alexander Koumoundouros as Prime Minister and Theodore Diliyannis as Foreign Minister.
3 March 1878	Peace Treaty of San Stefano. In effect, this is not the final draft of the treaty but a text delineating the preliminary terms for peace. The treaty gives the impression that the dreams of the pan-Slavists are coming true. The terms of the treaty are overturned by the decisions of the Berlin Congress.
30 April 1878	Under pressure from the Great Powers, the London Protocol is signed specifying the concessions the Tsar is prepared to make. Among other concessions Russia accepts a European conference to settle the new status of the Balkans.
4 June 1878	Signature in Constantinople of a secret de-

fensive alliance pact by which the Ottoman Empire permits Britain to assume the administration of Cyprus and oversee its interests in Asia Minor, Syria and Armenia.

July 1878

Congress of Berlin, attended by representatives of the six Great Powers and the Ottoman Empire. The Greek delegates, Theodore Diliyannis and Alexander Rangavis (then Ambassador in Berlin), are admitted only as observers. On 5 July, the Greek memorandum is debated without the country's participation. Under intense pressure from the Ottoman Empire, the Greek claims for the annexation of Epirus, Thessaly and Crete receive an unfair treatment. The treaty is finally signed on 13 July 1878.

30 October 1878

Signature of the Halepa Pact: Crete is granted autonomy, and the revolt of 1868 comes to an end. The agreement is the basis for a new *firman* making certain amendments to the 'Organic Law' of 1868.

6 February 1879

Greek and Ottoman delegations meet in Preveza to determine the new borders on the basis of the thirteenth protocol of the Berlin Congress, containing the terms of the Greek memorandum. Negotiations with the Ottoman Empire reach an impasse because the Ottoman Empire considers the thirteenth protocol non-binding. As a result the Greek government recalls its delegates. Negotiations (under the supervision of the Great Powers) recommence in Constantinople in August, but talks break down in December 1879.

1880

The emergence of administrations well-disposed towards Greece in both France and Britain, and the Ottomans' refusal to apply the thirteenth Protocol of the Berlin Congress, leads to a conference of ambassadors. The joint ambassadorial conference which excluded the interested parties, namely Greece and the Ottoman Empire, aims at delineating the Greek-Turkish frontiers. The failure of the Ottoman Empire to comply with the decision of the Great Powers of July 2, 1880, which adhered to the thirteenth protocol, and Greek military mobilisation, would have lead to new hostilities in the Balkans had Bismarck and Gladstone not intervened.

1881-1908   The Greek resistance in Macedonia counters Bulgarian penetration and prevents the armed *comitadjis* (Bulgarian nationalists) from eradicating the Greek element.

24 May 1881   Accepting a joint British and German plan, the Ottoman Empire gives ground and signs a convention (in Constantinople) settling the new Greek-Turkish borders. Thessaly and Arta are incorporated into Greece.

18 June 1881   Bismarck and the ambassadors of Austria and Russia sign a secret treaty in Berlin on a neutral position of the Powers (Germany, Russia and Austro-Hungary) towards the Ottoman Empire in the event of war.

2 July 1881   Under pressure from the Great Powers, the Ottoman Empire is compelled to sign the final Constantinople Convention settling the question that had arisen three years earlier and grants to Greece the greater part of Thessaly, the Punta fortress, and the region of Arta.

20 March 1882   Italy, Germany and Austria sign the Triple Alliance (against France and Russia), which remains in force until the early part of the First World War influencing important international issues for more than thirty years.

6 September 1885	The coup d' état in Philippopolis results in the complete absorption of Eastern Rumelia by Bulgaria. Public opinion in Greece is outraged and demands the implementation of the decisions reached at the Congress of Berlin. Faced with the threat of a new war between Greece and the Ottoman Empire, the Great Powers (with the exception of France) decide to implement a sea blockade against Greece on 26 April, 1886. Diliyannis resigns, Trikoupis assumes the premiership again and demobilises the Greek army. Peace is restored in the Balkans.
1887	Signature of three secret treaties through the exchange of notes, between Britain and Italy (February), Britain and Austria (March), and Italy and Spain (May).
April 1887	War looms between France and Germany.
March 1890	Bismarck is forced to resign. Franco-Russian rapprochement.
1892	The Russian and French General Staff sign a defensive military pact against the Triple Alliance. The pact is to remain in force for the duration of the Triple alliance. In 1900 the pact is extended to cover the eventuality of a British attack on either France or Russia.
1893	Foundation of the Internal Macedonian Revolutionary Organisation (IMRO), with the slogan of 'Macedonia for the Macedonians'.
1894	Both Tsar Alexander IIII and President Carnot of France die. The Franco-Russian alliance, however, survives signaling the end of German hegemony and the restoration of the balance of power in Europe. This is considered the most significant development for the period.
1895	Under pressure from the Western Powers,

Sultan Abdulhamit issues a *firman* appointing Karatheodoris, a Greek Christian, as governor of Crete. A year later he is replaced by an Ottoman pasha resulting in a rapidly deteriorating explosive situation.

1895   A Supreme Macedonian Committee is set up in Sofia. The armed struggle for the annexation of Macedonia begins.

1896   The first modern Olympic Games are held in Athens.

1897   Massacres of the Christian population in Crete oblige the Greek Consul in Chania to request that troops and a fleet be sent to the island. The Great Powers react to the threat of hostilities between Greece and the Ottoman Empire by blockading (3 February) the coast of the island and guaranteeing its autonomy.

April 1897   War between Greece and the Ottoman Empire breaks out. The Greek forces are defeated in Thessaly.

4 December 1897   Peace treaty between Greece and the Ottoman Empire is signed in Constantinople. Greece is obliged to evacuate Thessaly, accept the autonomy of Crete with Prince George as governor, and pay war reparations to the Ottomans. The latter measure necessitates the installation of a financial control commission.

December 1898   Prince George, first High Commissioner of Crete, lands on the island.

18-19 May 1899   The First World Peace Conference. Delegates from 26 countries meet at The Hague and resolve to set up a Permanent Court of Arbitration.

1904   Rapprochement between France and Britain, partly as a result of a change in the previously pro-German stance of Britain.

1904	Entente Cordiale is signed (Great Britain & France)
10 March 1905	The rising of Therissos in Crete is led by Eleftherios Venizelos. Prince George is succeeded as High Commissioner by the moderate Alexander Zaimis (Sept. 1906).
June 1908	The Young Turk revolution takes place.
1909	Abdulhamit is overthrown and replaced by Mohammed V. The Ottoman Constitution is revised.
15 August 1909	Officers of the 'Military League' revolt at Goudi. They invite Venizelos from Crete to come to Athens as their adviser.
30 August 1910	Venizelos achieves a sweeping victory in the polls.
2 July 1911	A new (revised) Constitution comes into force in Greece.
1910-1911	Greek-Turkish relations deteriorate as a result of the high-handed activities of the Young Turk nationalist movement.
September 1911	Italy launches an attack on Cyrenaica and captures Tripolis.
29 September 1911	Italy declares war on the Ottoman Empire and occupies the Dodecanese (1912).
1912	Frenzied diplomatic activity in the Balkans leads to rapprochement among the Balkan countries and results into treaties of alliance between Greece, Serbia and Bulgaria. Rapprochement between Bulgaria and Montenegro is also achieved.
October 1912	Outbreak of the First Balkan War: the four Christian states of the Balkans (Bulgaria, Serbia, Montenegro and Greece) engage in hostilities against the Ottoman Empire.
26 October 1912	The Greek Army enters Thessaloniki in triumph and proclaims the liberation of the

	city. Liberation of the Aegean islands and Epirus follows.
3 December 1912	The 'Elli naval battle' is the first major Greek victory at sea during the First Balkan War. It is followed by other successes before the end of the War in 1913.
30 May 1913	Signature of the London Peace Treaty: the Ottoman Empire is compelled to cede to the Balkan allies all the territories west of the Enos-Midia line as well as Crete. The Great Powers assume responsibility for deciding the ultimate fate of the Aegean islands.
1 June 1913	Greece and Serbia sign a treaty of friendship and mutual defence which establishes the common borders of the two countries and guarantees the sovereignty of their territorial acquisitions.
June 1913	Outbreak of the Second Balkan War: Bulgaria attacks Serbia and Greece.
July 1913	The Greek Army counter-attacks and advances as far as Kresna in Bulgaria. Roumania and the Ottomans take advantage of the circumstances to recover territory from Bulgaria.
10 August 1913	Signature of the Treaty of Bucharest brings the Second Balkan War to an end.
29 September 1913	The Treaty of Constantinople settles the Bulgarian-Turkish border.
November 1913	Signature of a bilateral agreement determining the Montenegro-Serbia border.
14 November 1913	Signarure of the Athens Convention between Greece and the Ottoman Empire: peaceful relations between the two belligerents are restored.
17 December 1913	The Florence Protocol defines the borders between Greece and Albania.
13 February 1914	The Great Powers send a note to Greece

	confirming the cession to Greece of the Aegean islands under Greek occupation (with the exception of Imbros, Tenedos and Castellorizo), on the condition that the Greek Army evacuates territory awarded to Albania by the Florence Protocol of 17 December 1913.
16 February 1914	The Ottoman Empire replies to the note issued by the Great Powers on 13 February.
17 February 1914	Northern Epirus declared autonomous.
21 February 1914	Greece replies to the note issued by the Great Powers on 13 February.
24 April 1914	In a new note to Greece, the Great Powers pledge to exercise friendly influence on the Ottoman Empire over its attitude towards Greek sovereignty over the Aegean islands.
17 May 1914	Corfu Protocol: the provinces of Korytsa and Argyrokastro gain privileges tantamount to autonomy.
28 July 1914	The assassination of Franz Ferdinand in Sarajevo leads Austria to declare war on Serbia: outbreak of the First World War.
30 October 1914	Ottoman naval units enter the Black Sea and shell Russian ports. The Entente issues an ultimatum to the Ottoman Empire, which comes into the War on the side of the Central Powers.
6 March 1915	Venizelos resigns and Dimitrios Gounaris forms a government. A chain of events raise serious constitutional questions splitting the country in two factions.
13 June 1915	Venizelos emerges victorious from the elections.
1 October 1915	British Army units land in Thessaloniki amid intense diplomatic negotiations with Athens, and against the background of the national rift between Venizelos and the King. The

	Allies aimed to force Greece to abandon neutrality as they anticipated a Bulgarian attack against Serbia.
4 October 1915	Venizelos gains the approval of Parliament - with a majority of 37 votes in favour of - for military aid to Serbia. On the following day, King Constantine demands his resignation and gives Alexander Zaimis the mandate to form an administration.
19 December 1915	Venizelos abstains from the elections and forms an extra-parliamentary opposition.
29 August 1916	Venizelist officers carry out the 'National Defence' revolt.
25 September 1916	At a particularly difficult time for Greece, Venizelos sails to Crete, and raises the flag of revolt. On 5 October he arrives in Thessaloniki, taking over the leadership of the National Defence movement and on 9 October sets up a pro-Entente provisional government. Greece is effectively split into two different states.
8 December 1916	The Allies declare a blockade on the part of Greece under royalist control.
6 April 1917	America declares war on Germany and sends troops to join the Entente forces.
12 June 1917	King Constantine abdicates in favour of his son Alexander and goes into voluntary exile.
27 June 1917	Venizelos reinstated as Prime Minister.
29 June 1917	Greece enters the war on the side of the Entente (the official declaration of war, however, does not take place until 24 November).
October 1917	The Russian revolution. The Bolsheviks led by Lenin seize power.
December 1917	Brest-Litovsk peace talks begin between Russia and Germany.
8 January 1918	Woodrow Wilson announced his Fourteen Points.

3 March 1918	Signature of the Brest-Litovsk Peace Treaty.
16 July 1918	The last Tsar of Russia and his family are shot in Siberia.
30 October 1918	The Entente Powers and the Ottoman Empire sign armistice at Mudros; the terms are especially harsh for the Ottomans.
7 January 1919	Allied troops, including Greek forces, land at Odessa.
28 April 1919	Signature of the treaty setting up the League of Nations and heralding the five peace treaties (Versailles, St. Germain, Trianon, Neuilly & Sèvres) which followed. The League of Nations is convened on 10 January 1920.
15 May 1919	Greek troops land at Smyrna. Venizelos has received authorisation from Britain and France, which saw their interests in Asia Minor threatened by Italy.
21 May 1919	Aristidis Stergiadis, former Governor-General of Epirus and an enthusiastic supporter of the policies of Venizelos, assumes the position of High Commissioner in Smyrna.
28 June 1919	The Treaty of Versailles, the first of the peace treaties after the end of the war is signed.
21 July 1919	A Supreme Command consisting of an equal number of representatives from each of the Great Powers is set up to control an apparently unstable situation in Smyrna.
29 July 1919	Venizelos-Tittoni Agreement: Italy accepts the cession of Northern Epirus and the Dodecanese (except Rhodes) to Greece. In return, Greece recognises Italian claims in Avlona and Asia Minor.
10 September 1919	The Treaty of St. Germain, the second peace, is signed.
12 November 1919	In a letter from French Prime Minister Clemenceau, the Allies inform Venizelos that the Greek military presence in Smyrna is to

be regarded as purely temporary. The position of the Allies was not homogeneous. There were those who undermined Greece, such as Italy, those, such as France who were opposed to Greece and those who adopted a passive stance.

27 November 1919
The Treaty of Neuilly, was the third treaty that was concluded after the end of the war. The treaty concerned mainly Bulgaria and Greece. Under this treaty, Bulgaria renounces all rights on Western Thrace, which in turn is awarded to Greece.

4 June 1920
The fourth peace treaty: the Treaty of Trianon, dissolves the Austro-Hungarian Empire disturbing the balance of power in Europe.

June 1920
The Greek Army receives permission from the Allies to occupy Eastern Thrace.

25 July 1920
Occupation of Adrianople.

30 July 1920
Assassination attempt on Venizelos at the Lyon railway station. An attack of anti-Venizelist newspapers and politicians breaks out in Athens. Ion Dragoumis, a leader of the anti-Venizelist party is arrested by paramilitary troops and executed on the spot.

10 August 1920
The fifth of the peace treaties: the Treaty of Sèvres, under which Greece also receives Eastern Thrace as far as the Chataldja lines and the European shore of the Dardanelles. Turkey recognises Greek sovereignty over the Aegean islands, with the exception of the Dodecanese, which together with Castellorizo are ceded to Italy. It is also decided that Smyrna and the area around it should be administered by Greece under the nominal sovereignty of the Sultan. There is provision for a plebiscite in five years' time. The Treaty was never enforced.

25 October 1920	Death of King Alexander.
14 November 1920	Parliamentary elections result in the crushing defeat of Venizelos.
19 December 1920	Upon the defeat of Venizelos, King Constantine returns to Athens after three years in exile.
June 1921	The Greek Army launches a major offensive in Asia Minor. Afyon Karahissar, Kiutaya and Eskishehir come under Greek control.
26 August 1922	Kemal Atatürk, at the head of the Turkish Army, launches a successful counterattack. Greece, abandoned by its allies, is defeated, Smyrna is burned, and the Greek population of Asia Minor is expelled and uprooted from its homeland (18 September). On 27 August Archbishop Chrysostomos is lynched by a Turkish mob upon the orders of the Turkish authoriries.
27 September 1922	A military coup d'état overthrows the King who abdicates and dies at Palermo on 11 January 1923. On 31 October, the six officers and politicians held responsible for the Asia Minor disaster are court-martial.
11 October 1922	Armistice signed at Mudania: Greece recognises Turkish claims on Smyrna and Eastern Thrace and undertakes to withdraw its troops beyond the river Evros within 15 days.
20 November 1922	The Lausanne Conference begins. The Greek delegation is headed by Eleftherios Venizelos. The Conference proposes that the Greek border should be pushed back to the river Evros. A compulsory exchange of populations follows.
28 November 1922	The six politicians held responsible for the national disaster in Asia Minor are executed.
23 July 1923	The Peace Treaty and a Convention on the regime of the Straits are signed in Lausanne.

31 August 1923	Mussolini takes the assasination of Italian general Tellini as a pretext for bombing and occupying Corfu.
27 September 1923	Under pressure from Britain and in the face of intense reaction from Greece, the Italian fleet withdraws from Corfu.
25 March 1924	The National Assembly under, Alexander Papanastasiou declares Greece a Republic.
1 December 1925	The texts of the Locarno Pact (15-16 Oct.) are signed in London. The pact provides for Germany's entrance to the League of Nations The Foreign Ministers of Britain, France and Germany (Chamberlain, Briand and Stresemann) play a pivotal role in the signature of the treaty and as recognition for their accomplishment they receive the Nobel peace prize.
17 December 1925	A Russian-Turkish neutrality pact is signed in Paris; protocols follow in 1929, 1931 and 1935, and a naval agreement in 1931. Russia's policy of reconciliation in the Balkans initiates a period of tacit truce in the area.
24 December 1925	A Russian-Turkish agreement in the nature of an anti-Locarno pact is the answer to the West's settlement with Germany.
25 June 1925	General Pangalos imposes a dictatorship and, as sole candidate, is elected President of the Republic. Pangalos is overthrown (22 August 1926) by a military coup led by General Kondylis, and Admiral Pavlos Koundouriotis is once more installed as President of the Republic. «Oecumenical» all-party government is established in 1926.
27 November 1926	Italy and Albania sign the Tirana Agreement; Albania becomes an Italian protectorate.
May 1928	Italy and Turkey sign a pact of friendship.
19 August 1928	Venizelos returns to the political scene,

	winning 223 seats in Parliament at elections held on the first-past-the-post system.
1928 - 1932	Venizelos solidifies the policy of good relations with the Great Powers of Europe and the neighbouring states. Special emphasis is given to the Greco-Turkish rapprochement and friendship. Greek-Turkish Treaty signed by Venizelos and Atatürk (in Ancara 30 Oct. 1930).
1929	The pact of friendship signed by Italy and Yugoslavia in 1926 expires and is not renewed.
4 January 1932	Italy and Turkey sign an agreement on the islets located between Anatolia and Castellorizo as well as the island of Kara Ada. The territorial waters surrounding these islets are delineated, since sovereignty over them had been the subject of dispute between Italy and Turkey.
April 1932	The defeat of Venizelos at the March elections creates political instability and leads to new elections in September of the same year.
28 December 1932	Italy and Turkey sign an agreement further delineating the remaining sea border between the two countries. This part of the frontier had never been disputed between the two countries.
January 1933	Hitler comes to power in Germany.
16 February 1933	The charter of the Little Entente is signed.
6 June 1933	A second assassination attempt on the life of Venizelos.
15 July 1933	Britain, France, Germany and Italy sign a final text in Rome. It is based on an Italian draft which originally proposed revision of the peace treaties still in force by the League of Nations. The agreement became known as

	the Collaboration and Consultation Pact. The pact was never enforced.
24 September 1933	The Foreign Ministers of Greece and Turkey (Maximos and Rushdi Aras) sign a pact of guarantee between their two countries in Ankara. Greece and Turkey attempt, unsuccessfully, to extend their co-operation to include other Balkan countries such as Bulgaria and Yugoslavia.
October 1933	Germany leaves the League of Nations.
9 February 1934	Signature in Athens of the Balkan Entente between Greece, Yugoslavia, Roumania and Turkey. The pact is a mutual guarantee of the frontiers of the Balkan States.
21 November 1934	Signature in Ankara of the Balkan Entente Charter.
18 June 1935	Signature of the Anglo-German Naval Agreement in London by which the latter is permitted to re-arm to a proportion of up to 35% of the British fleet.
3 October 1935	Italy attacks Abyssinia. The war lasts seven months and ends by terminating Abyssinian independence (5 May 1936).
10 October 1935	In an atmosphere of intransigence created by the anti-Venizelists, a coup takes place and Kondylis forms an administration.
25 November 1935	King George II returns to Greece after a referendum held on 3 November.
13 April 1936	Prime Minister C. Demertzis dies. I. Metaxas assumes the premiership on the same day.
20 July 1936	Signature of the Treaty of Montreux, by which Turkey acquires complete political and military control over the Straits.
4 August 1936	Metaxas abolishes parliamentary democracy and declares a dictatorship. As the Second World War looms closer, the foreign policy

	and diplomacy of Metaxas and the King are orientated towards Britain and France.
1937	Pacts of friendship between Bulgaria and Yugoslavia (20 January) and Italy and Yugoslavia (25 March), are signed in Belgrade.
February 1937	A Military Convention is signed in Bucharest supplementing the Balkan Pact. The idea of a Balkan collaboration belongs to the reformist Greek politician Alexandros Papanastasiou.
27 April 1938	A supplementary treaty between Greece and Turkey is signed in Athens. The treaty guarantees neutrality in the event that either state is attacked by a third country.
31 July 1938	Signature of an agreement between Bulgaria and the Balkan Entente. Bulgaria undertakes not to use force, while the Entente agrees to release Bulgaria from its obligation (under the Treaty of Neuilly) not to increase its armed forces.
29 September 1938	Hitler, Mussolini, Chamberlain and Daledier attend the Munich Conference which provides for the dismemberment of Czechoslovakia.
7 April 1939	Italian troops invade Albania.
22 May 1939	The 'Pact of Steel' is signed - Hitler's greatest personal success and a triumph for Germany.
23 August 1939	The Nazi-Soviet Non-Aggression Pact is signed and created preconditions for the attack on Poland.
1 September 1939	The Germans and the Soviets invade Poland without a prior declaration of war. Warsaw surrenders. Ribbentrop and Molotov sign (in Moscow) a pact of friendship which delineates the borders by three secret protocols.
3 September 1939	Britain and France declare war on Germany.
10 May 1940	German troops cross the Belgian border. Luxembourg capitulates, followed by the

	Netherlands on 15 May and Belgium on 28 May.
26 May - 4 June 1940	The evacuation of Dunkirk codenamed 'Dynamo' is successfully conducted.
5 June 1940	German offensive renewed; capture of Paris (14 June).
10 June 1940	Italy declares war against France and Britain.
22 June 1940	France and Germany sign a cease-fire agreement.
24 June 1940	France and Italy sign a cease-fire agreement.
3 July 1940	On July 1 the British war cabinet decides to destroy the French Fleet lest it be used by the Germans. The operation took place on July 3 and it led to a rift in Anglo-French relations.
15 September 1940	The end of the 'phony war'. The aerial bombardment of Britain begins. Britain puts up valiant resistance to Hitler's 'Sea-Lion' and 'Eagle' operations resulting in Hitler's first major defeat.
27 September 1940	The Tripartite Pact is signed between Germany, Italy and Japan.
28 October 1940	Italy declares war on Greece, a few months after entering the War on the side of the Axis.
14 November 1940	After first fighting off the Italian offensive from Albania, Greece counter-attacks and on 22 November Greek troops enter Korytsa, on 6 December they take Aghioi Saranta, and on 8 December they occupy Argyrokastro.
19-20 January 1941	Operation Marita is finalised at a conference between Italy and Germany held at Salzburg.
17 February 1941	Bulgaria and Turkey sign a non-aggression pact.
9 March 1941	Italy launches its spring offensive.
25 March 1941	As the Italian offensive against Greece comes to a halt, the quisling Yugoslavian puppet regimes accede to the Tripartite Pact (Axis).
6 April 1941	German forces attack Yógoslavia. Thessalo-

	niki is captured on 9 April, and Athens is occupied on April 27.
20 May 1941	Beginning of the German attack on Crete. The King and the government sail by submarine for Alexandria.
31 May 1941	Crete falls. The whole of Greece is under German occupation.
22 June 1941	Operation Barbarossa: Germany attacks the Soviet Union.
7 July 1941	After receiving a cool reception from the Egyptian authorities, the King and the government-in-exile under Tsouderos make their way to Durban in South Africa.
25 August 1941	The King, the Prime Minister and the Governor of the Bank of Greece leave Cape Town for London, where numerous other governments-in-exile are also based. Some of the Cabinet - notably the war ministers - remain in Cairo.
7 December 1941	Japan attacks the United States Pacific Fleet at Pearl Harbour.
June 1942	On the invitation of President F. D. Roosevelt, King George and the Prime Minister visit the United States and brief the Americans on Greek national issues.
23 Aug. 1942-31 Jan. 1943	Siege of Stalingrad.
14-24 January 1943	The Casablanca Conference.
10 July 1943	Allied landing in Sicily.
25 July 1943	Mussolini resigns. Field-Marshal Badoglio receives the mandate by King Victor Emmanuel to form an administration.
Mid-August 1943	The Quebec Conference.
8 September 1943	Italy capitulates and is placed under Allied Administration Control.
9 September 1943	Allies land at Salerno.
29 September 1943	Signature of the Badoglio-Eisenhower Pact.
13 October 1943	Italy declares war on Germany.

Last quarter of 1943	Beginning of the 'first round' in the Greek Civil War.
26 April 1944	George Papandreou appointed Prime Minister-in-exile.
6 June 1944	Operation Overlord (D-Day). The Allies land in Normandy.
20 July 1944	Unsuccessful attempt to assassinate Hitler.
21 August 1944	Papandreou meets Churchill in Rome; it is decided to move the Greek government to Italy.
8 Sept.-3 Oct. 1944	The Greek Mountain Brigade is distinguished at the Battle of Rimini.
11-16 September 1944	Second Anglo-American Conference in Quebec, code named 'Octagon'
24 September 1944	First British troops land in Greece.
8 October 1944	On their way to Moscow, Churchill and Eden meet Papandreou in Naples. The question of removing the Bulgarians from Macedonia and Thrace is discussed. The British clamour for an early return of the King, but give ground when Papandreou threatens to resign.
9-20 October 1944	The percentage agreement between Churchill and Stalin calls for the division of the Balkans into spheres of influence.
12 October 1944	The Germans evacuate Athens.
18 October 1944	G. Papandreou, the Greek government, and General Scobie land at Piraeus. In a historic speech in Syntagma Square, Papandreou talks of the need to reconstruct Greece and refers to the national issues of Northern Epirus and the Dodecanese.
4-11 February 1945	Yalta Conference. The second Big Three summit takes place in the Crimea.
7 May 1945	Unconditional surrender of Germany.
26 June 1945	Charter of the United Nations and statute of the International Court of Justice signed in San Francisco.

5 July 1945	The Labour Party wins the British elections and Churchill retires to Biarritz for a brief rest. The British election results affect internal developments in Greece.
6 August 1945	The first atomic bomb explodes over Hiroshima.
9 August 1945	The second atomic bomb is dropped on Nagasaki.
13 September 1945	Unconditional surrender of Japan.
September 1945	Archbishop Damaskinos pays a triumphant visit to Rhodes; the Dodecanese islands, recently liberated, are occupied by British troops.
1 November 1945	After a lengthy governmental crisis during which Themistoclis Sophoulis and Sophoclis Venizelos tried to form administrations, a government under Panayotis Kanellopoulos is sworn in. A period of economic chaos follows, with weak governments under a strong British influence. Damaskinos, embarrassed by a British disclosure that he had asked for parliamentary elections to precede a referendum on the monarchy, resigns as Regent but in view of the critical situation remains in his post until the first post-election administration is sworn in.
22 November 1945	The Sophoulis Administration which consists largely of liberals is sworn in. A general amnesty is proclaimed and elections are announced to take place on 31 March 1946.
1 September 1946	A referendum on the future of the Greek monarchy results in 68% of the electorate voting in favour of restoration and a 32% against.
2 October 1946	Upon the return of King George, Tsaldaris resigns, and he immediately forms a new administration. At the Paris Peace Confer-

ence of 1946, Tsaldaris puts forward Greek demands for the incorporation of Northern Epirus and the Dodecanese islands to Greece. On the first claim he encountered the strong resistance of the new Communist leader of Albania Enver Xoxha. He was much more successful with regards to the Greek claim to the Dodecanese. The islands were turned over to Greek sovereignty under the Paris Peace Treaty with Italy on 10 February 1947. It was during this period that Greece would witness the retreat of Britain and the increase of American power in the region.

INDEX